Arkansas Food

Arkansas Food

SMOKED SIRLOIN · garden greens · CAVENDER'S · FUDGE · Trout Pate · SMOKED MEATS · Jerky · Sweet Corn · BEEF · pumpkins · MILK · Dang Good Pie · Pepper Jelly · World's Second Best Pizza · Rice & Brown Gravy · Old Fashioned Chocolate Fried Pies · FRIED CHICKEN & SPAGHETTI · HAM · TURKEY · Green Tomato Relish · RICE · Fried Rice · PIGMEAT SANDWICHES · RIBS · Rabbits · EXCALIBURGER · Buffalo · Cornbread in Buttermilk · Turnip Greens · Chicken Gizzards · Quail · Jelly · Company's Comin' Pie · Chocolate Gravy · Sweetest Watermelons · Strawberry Shortcake · Pizza Burger · Big Donuts · Pho · Spinach · Blackberries · OATS · OZARKIES · Arkansas Blackapples · Chocolate Rolls · REUBEN SANDWICH · CATFISH · GAR · French Dip · Wine · Cathead Biscuits · Honey · Ice Cream · Butter Roll · POT LIKKER · ELVIS ATE HERE · Diner Food · GRAPES · BACON · Fried Pies · SOP · Ginormous Burgers · Fried Pickles · Bright Red Weiners · Biscuit Pudding · CHICKEN · Uncle Roman · THE STOBY · Play-De-Do · Italian Roll · Strawberries · Frito Chili Pie · Oyster Supper · RED GRAVY · Strawberry Cobbler · Sweet Potatoes · EDAMAME · Cheese Dip · Little Rock Roll · Fried Cabbage · Huge Freakin' Cinnamon Rolls · Crapple · Sweet Potato Pie · Hubcap Burgers · More Rice · Mr. Jones and his Pork Sandwiches · Trace Creek Potatoes · Cornbread · DUCK · PASTA · Corned Beef Sandwiches · Chess Pie · Cotton Blossoms · Peaches · BARBECUE · Pimento · Pecans · Tamales · Poke Salat · Peanut Brittle · Cheese · Possum Pie · Crawdads · Sorghum Molasses · Best Coke in town · Butter Beans · Blueberries · Venison · Burger Joints · FRIED BOLOGNA SANDWICHES · Grapette · Big Honkin' Steaks · COON · Cream Gravy · Cushaw Pie · Sliced Red Tomatoes · Signal Rice · Biscuits · Turkey Fries · Watermelons · Muscadines · More BBQ · Butter Cake · EGGS · Smothered Chicken · Hush Puppies · PORK · TAMALES AND PIE · Collard Greens · Smoked Turkeys · Pink Tomatoes · SPUDNUTS · Mayhaw Jelly · Bean Dip · PurpleHull Peas · Armadillo Eggs · soybeans

Kat Robinson

The A to Z of Eating in The Natural State

TONTI PRESS

Published by Tonti Press
Little Rock, Arkansas

Cover image: PurpleHull peas in a bucket at the Emerson PurpleHull Pea Festival and World Champion Rotary Tiller Races, 2017

Back cover: Arkansas Blackapples and Stoby's cheese dip

Spine: Grapes in the vineyard at sunrise at Post Familie Vineyard in Altus

All photography by Kat Robinson except where noted.

First published December 2018

Manufactured in the United States of America

ISBN 978-0-9998734-2-7

Library of Congress Control Number: 2018911879

To my mom, Kitty Waldon, for letting me loose in her kitchen and allowing me to create anything I desired from what I found as a child, fostering my curiosity in the culinary arts.

For my daughter, Hunter Robinson.
It's your turn in the kitchen now.

FOREWORD

I met Kat Robinson back in 2010 in Little Rock when she strolled into Ashley's at The Capital, the restaurant where I was working at the time. Kat stopped by that day to learn all about the food we were cooking. Our scheduled half hour interview turned into three hours of lively conversation that veered off from what we were cooking up at Ashley's to what was cooking in kitchens across the state.

It was during that first meeting that I realized that Kat's curiosity and passion about all things Arkansas food is backed up by her deep knowledge of it. No one has clocked more miles traveling to every part of the state's 75 counties in search of recipes or culinary treasures. And yet, Kat continues to uncover hidden culinary gems in the Natural State from mom and pop restaurants to church potlucks to grand culinary haunts.

Today she is my personal go-to when I have questions about the food of our state, and that's because no other person I know has lived and breathed the Arkansas food story more than Kat.

Kat was born in Wilmington, North Carolina, but her parents were both from Arkansas, and she arrived here in The Natural State when she was still very small. Her passion for the state's culinary offerings began early. Ask Kat about the food she grew up eating and she'll detail memories of her grandma's fried chocolate hand pies, hand-pounded country fried venison steaks and the fresh tomatoes from the garden.

As a writer, Kat has generously shared the stories of Arkansas' food and eateries with the readers of national publications like Lonely Planet and Food Network Magazine as well as in countless statewide publications. She has even written two books about Arkansas pie! And each tale is a celebration of Arkansas fare, like chocolate gravy, cheese dip, Coursey smoked hams and Cavenders Greek Seasoning.

Over the years, as Southern food became all the rage, Arkansas didn't get much of the spotlight. But that is changing and finally, the delicious food of the Natural State is getting its due in large part thanks to Kat. And Kat makes the case that being late to the party lets you choose how to arrive.

In *Arkansas Food: The A to Z of Eating in The Natural State,* Kat has written a book that catalogs the Arkansas food story, so the next time I call upon her with a question about a recipe or local ingredient, I'm sure she'll tell me that if I really want to know all I need to do is consult my copy of her book.

Matthew McClure
Executive Chef, The Hive at 21c

INTRODUCTION

What is Arkansas Food?

The question seemed innocuous when it was first presented. I was interviewing a chef in his new restaurant, learning how he'd sourced not only ingredients for his dishes but ideas for recipes after spending some time out and about in the state. When he turned that question back to me, I didn't have an answer.

It was autumn, 2007. I had just left a career, twelve years as a local affiliate news producer. I knew I wanted to write, and had started a website called Tie Dye Travels to keep my writing chops up. I thought I'd do what every other former TV producer in our market seemed to do - go into marketing or non-profit work, be a spokeswoman or communications associate, that sort of thing. I was picking up a little work here and there writing for checkout magazines the ones you pick up for free at the grocery store, trying to make a little money while I figured out what I was going to do.

But there was this question... a question I wasn't ready to answer. I wasn't certain anyone was. I lived in a city where most meals were taken outside the home. Little Rock, at the time, was a land of a few culinary jewels buried in a sea of chains. While there have always been a goodly number of lunch counters and dinettes for meat-and-three plates, we were at the time struggling. There were standouts like Trio's and Cajun's Wharf and Faded Rose, but for every one of those there were three Dixie Cafés (a now-gone Arkansas Southern food chain) and eight

Taco Bells. There was the farmers' market at Ottenheimer Hall in the River Market on Tuesdays and Saturdays in the warmer months, but past that I knew of only a handful of places to get fresh, locally grown fruits and vegetables. Pulaski Technical College had just really rolled its program into the Arkansas Culinary School. There was this guy by the name of Jody Hardin who was trying to get together local farmers for a farm-to-home program featuring our native foods. And there was the man who tossed that question back to me, Chef Lee Richardson, who'd been recruited by the Stephenses to be the executive chef at Ashley's at the Capital, the venerable restaurant that would re-open alongside the famed Capital Hotel that year.

I blathered on a bit with bits of trivia - Belzoni, Mississippi was the Catfish Capital of the World, Bradley County Pink tomatoes were both Arkansas's state fruit and vegetable, the incredible chocolate at Martin Greer's Candies in Gateway, the sweetest watermelons I'd ever had and where they could be found around Cave City. But I really didn't have a definitive answer.

I needed to get one.

I learned early in my writing career that if I wrote about food, I wouldn't starve. The opportunity to choose what I wanted to write about, to sate my curiosity and find answers, played into my ideas as a journalist. The timing could not have been better; Arkansas was blooming for the first time as a food lover's destination. Our low cost-of-living, spread of rural farmlands, abundance of water, variety of terrain and plethora of entrepreneurs compiled a perfect culinary storm. Upstart operations blossomed in Little Rock and North Little Rock, Rogers and Bentonville, Eureka Springs, Hot Springs and Conway. A new crop of culinarians, chefs and farmers cross-pollinated ideas about our foodstuffs to invigorate our spankin' new 21st century cuisine.

At the same time, a wave of nostalgia and a general quest for historical grounding for these culinary pursuits was beginning to crest. We as Arkansawyers started finding ourselves curious for more than what the ingredients could create. We wanted to discover what we'd lost in those years where franchises and chain operations had supplanted our local-grown eateries. We craved the flavors of our rural youth. We just needed to figure out how to get back there.

My journey to find these things has taken me to kitchen counters and farmyards, to greasy spoons and white linen soirées, to community festivals and dinners and truck stops and dairy bar windows. Assumptions were wiped away with gravy-soiled napkins. I dived into decades old church cookbooks and listened to folks chat at the next table. There were no textbooks for my scholarship; the residents of this state were my instructors.

What did I learn? Arkansas is a stubborn, hang-on-by-your-teeth subsistence land that adapts to weather, new folks and the lay of the land. Its cuisine isn't Southern or Appalachian or Midwestern, though elements of all of these things are evidenced by our communal meals. Its regional specialties are tied tight to its geographical holding place; my own experience of country fried venison and sugared rice as breakfast was certainly as strange to my Delta friends' dinners of wild duck and rice as theirs was to me. Searcy County's chocolate rolls, an expected everyday dessert when visiting my brother's side of the family, seems far more exotic now that I realize they're found nowhere else.

We're innovators - and we always have been. Look at Mountain Valley Water, where the product literally comes up from the ground whole and ready to consume, and how it's been marketed over the years. Or Benjamin Tyndle Fooks, who came up with thick, sweet flavored syrups and sold them out of the trunk of his car to put in carbonated water, thus creating Grapette and Orangette. Or the chemist Robert Switzer, who while working at the Atkins Pickle Company to develop pickle flavors, created the Tomolive, a tiny pickled tomato that's a remarkable garnish for mixed drinks. Outlandish marketing and inspired creation is in our genetic makeup.

Granny's Butter Bowl
at Pea Farm Bistro in
Cabot.

Arkansas food is far more than fried pickles, cheese dip and chocolate gravy, though we will lay claim to all three and celebrate them ecstatically. It's our desire to take that first bite of a Johnson county peach in the hottest part of summer, or to whip up any number of gravies to go along with the preferred meat or starch of the day. It's our summer plate, our ancestral go-to that hearkens back to sitting down briefly at lunch to consume just a bit of what we'd just picked from the garden, to savor quietly before resting during the hottest bit of the day. It's the stew of culinary traditions absorbed in whole by a state awash in generations of immigrants from across the globe, assimilated into our culinary lexicon and humbly shared, rarely bragged upon, happily consumed.

This book isn't all there is to Arkansas food. It's an intellectual breaking of the bread of information, morsels of life here, stories shared and origins remembered. I've been immersed in this cuisine all my life, and I've studied it intently these past 11 years, and I still feel I've just scratched the surface. The photos are mostly mine, from all these years of seeking out information for stories to share. Some are those of my partner, Grav Weldon, who came on board in 2010 to shoot what I wrote about and, who at first, questioned my sanity over the possibility that there was indeed an Arkansas cuisine. He too is now a convert.

Crawfish hush puppy at
Rebel Kettle in Little Rock.

There are also postcards, historical photographs and recipes from all over the state, gleaned from church and community cookbooks and from the restaurants themselves, captured instructions for edibles that deserve not to be lost in time. Of the 138 recipes between this book's covers, you'll find five completely different recipes for cheese dip, a handful featuring wild game, and a bounty of side dishes. I didn't start out to write a cookbook, but when word got around that I wanted to encapsulate Arkansas's cuisine, the recipes were given.

The photos, for a great part, do not match the recipes. Some do. What you'll see captured in these pages are images of actual real, unposed and completely edible food, the way it's brought to table. There's no airbrushing here, no marketing techniques utilizing non-edible components. These are the dishes you'll encounter when you visit restaurants mentioned in this book.

Arkansas Food: The A to Z of Eating in The Natural State is meant not to limit you, but to share some of the many facets of what it's like to eat and enjoy The Natural State, and to inspire you to try these delicacies yourself. Enjoy, be hungry, and find your own culinary path here.

Kat Robinson
Little Rock
November 29, 2018

APPLE BUTTER

A condiment popular as a breakfast sweet and sometimes as a sandwich spread, this is a concoction of apples and spices that's been rendered down and canned for future consumption.

Apple butter is manufactured by several purveyors in Arkansas, notably House of Webster and The Pancake Shop. The latter serves its version in metal cups alongside housemade grape jelly with every breakfast. It's also a component in the family-style dinners at the Monte Ne Inn Chicken Restaurant near Rogers, where it's served alongside fresh baked loaves of bread. Apple butter is delectable on biscuits with butter but can also serve as a lovely counterpoint to ham or other smoked meats.

This recipe by Cynthia Lewis appears in the *Family Restaurant Collection at All Souls Church Ladies Aid* from the Scott community, printed in 1981.

Apple Butter

5 cups apple pulp, made from 3 lbs. apples (preferably Jonathan), unpeeled

2 1/2 cups sugar
1/4 teaspoon ground allspice

Dash of salt
2 cups water
1 teaspoon cinnamon
1/8 teaspoon ground cloves
Dash of lemon juice

In heavy saucepan, put two cups water, dash of salt and lemon juice. Wash, core and quarter apples, dropping them into the lemon mixture. Simmer, covered, til apples are tender, adding a little more water if necessary. Put through colander, removing skins. Measure five cups pulp; add sugar and spices and simmer, uncovered, stirring frequently, about 15 minutes. Seal in clean jars, and refrigerate when cool. Yields five cups.

Apple butter on fresh baked bread at the Monte Ne Inn Chicken Restaurant near Rogers.

Apples for sale at the Bentonville Farmer's Market.

APPLES

Back at the beginning of the 20th century, Arkansas was actually known as the Apple State. Washington and Benton Counties were the two top apple-producing counties in the entire United States. Much was exported as whole fruit, but dehydrated fruit was also common from the area until 1920. At one point in 1895 there were 47 distilleries using apples to create vinegar and brandy in the area.

The earliest reports of apple crops in Arkansas comes from an 1822 reference in the *Arkansas Gazette*, noting the fruit was being grown west of Pulaski County on the farm of James Sevier Conway. Arkansas's hilly Ozarks region is prime for growing apples, thanks to an amenable climate and good drainage.

See also Blackapples.

University of Arkansas Special Collections

In 1930, a special confection known as Ruby's Apple Delight was created and sold by one Miss Ruby Mendenhall, an Extension Service economist in Rogers. Slices of apples were candied, covered in chocolate and sold to tourists and for special occasions.

ARKANSAS BACON

Most bacon sold in US stores today is made from pork bellies. "Arkansas-style" bacon is made from the Boston roast/shoulder of the hog. Most bacon offered for commercial sale in Arkansas is traditional bacon. Arkansas-style bacon is actually legislated, as seen here in the Arkansas Code of 1987.

20-60-102. Arkansas bacon.

(a)(1) The term "Arkansas bacon" shall not be used to identify any meat product other than the pork shoulder blade Boston roast prepared in the State of Arkansas in accordance with this section.

(2) Pork shoulder blade Boston roast prepared outside the State of Arkansas but in the manner prescribed by this section may be identified as "Arkansas-style bacon".

(b)(1) "Arkansas bacon" and "Arkansas-style bacon" are produced from the pork shoulder blade Boston roast by removing the neck bones and rib bones by cutting close to the underside of those bones, removing the blade bone or scapula, and removing the dorsal fat covering, including the skin or clear plate, and leaving no more than one-quarter inch (14 w) of the fat covering the roast.

(2)(A) The meat is then dry-cured with salt, sugar, nitrites, and spices, and smoked with natural smoke.

(B) The meat may not be injected or soaked in curing brine, nor may any artificial or liquid smoke be applied to the meat.

(3) The pork shoulder blade Boston roast includes the porcine muscle, fat, and bone cut interior of the second or third thoracic vertebrae and posterior of the atlas joint or first cervical vertebrae and dorsal of the center of the humerus bone.

(c) Any person who labels or otherwise identifies meat contrary to the provisions of this section shall be guilty of a violation punishable by a fine not to exceed one thousand dollars ($1,000).

Few purveyors smoke or utilize this style of bacon in practice today. One of those is Tusk and Trotter, a High South restaurant just off the square in downtown Bentonville. Chef Rob Nelson's operation celebrates all the parts of the pig, and serves the delicious delicacy of Arkansas bacon seen here.

Tusk & Trotter's Arkansas Bacon

1 cup Kosher salt
1/2 cup rib rub
4 Tablespoons pink salt

1 1/2 cups brown sugar, packed
1 1/2 cups sorghum sugar
30 pounds pork shoulder butt

Combine ingredients for rub. Rub down the shoulder butts and let rest at room temperature for 30 minutes. Before chilling, rub down again. Store in walk-in 7-10 days and rotate every other day. After curing process is complete, rinse off the cure with cold water. Pat shoulders dry and smoke at 200 degrees for 4 1/2 hours.

ARKANSAS CUMIN RICE

Particular to Arkansas County and even Arkansas City, where the White and Arkansas Rivers meet before they hit the Mississippi, this dish is a staple for generations of Arkansas Delta folk. This recipe comes from Paulette Thompson out of *Cornerstone Cookery* (1983). This is significantly different from Indian jeera rice.

1/3 cup chopped onion
1/4 cup chopped bell pepper
1 cup uncooked rice
2 Tablespoons bacon drippings or oil

2 cups beef broth
1 Tablespoon Worcestershire sauce
¾ teaspoon salt
¾ teaspoon cumin seed

Sauté onion, bell pepper and rice in bacon drippings or oil until rice is golden brown (use low heat and stir to prevent over-browning). Turn out into two-quart casserole. Bring beef broth to a boil and add to casserole. Add remaining ingredients. Stir well. Cover tightly with lid or foil and bake at 350 degrees for 30 minutes or until rice is tender and liquid is absorbed. Fluff lightly with fork before serving.

ARKANSAS EGGS BENEDICT

A variant breakfast dish served up in some areas of the state. Jonesboro food lover Christopher Wheeless describes it thusly:

"I grew up with it on toasted French bread, with a light layer of mayonnaise or Miracle Whip, lettuce or tomato; bacon or another fried meat that you'd prefer; fried bologna and a runny egg that when you were in the midst of eating the sandwich, it would burst open. And you'd use the sandwich and the bread and the rest of it to mop up the runny yolk as you eat it. It's awesome, it's nothing fancy. Growing up here in Arkansas, because our tomatoes are so good, the acidity of the tomato with that bacon fat or sausage fat with that fried bologna texture, smooth but it had some firmness to it, running over with the egg was absolutely delicious."

ARK-MEX

A product of post-World War II and 1950s new road travel desires, this blend of Arkansas produce and flavors with Mexican standards has influenced generations of restaurants, from Mexico Chiquito in the 1940s in Prothro Junction to Pancho's Mexican Restaurant in West Memphis in 1953; from The Oasis in Eureka Springs to Heights Taco and Tamale Company in Little Rock today.

Ark-Mex food is different from Mexican fare and from Tex-Mex, which tends to rely more on lard, cilantro and monolithic quesos. Ark-Mex bends more towards fresh tomatoes, ground beef and the homegrown cheese dip (*see* Cheese Dip, we'll talk about the Donnelly family's Little Mexico there). While Tex-Mex is all about the black bean these days, Ark-Mex shies towards the pinto bean, shredded Cheddar and American cheeses and chunky salsas.

In addition to those places listed above, many of our heritage restaurants both past and present based their menu on Ark-Mex - in particular, the now-gone El Cena Casa of Benton, the community favorite Taco Villa in Russellville, and to a lesser extent Paragould's Taco Rio.

And then there was Browning's. The Little Rock hacienda started serving customers in 1946. John Browning and his son-in-law, Boyd Montgomery, opened its doors shortly after the end of the second World War. It changed hands a few times over the years, but up through the early '00s it managed to maintain a certain flavor and atmosphere.

Original Browning's location. Photo courtesy Height's Taco and Tamale.

The original Browning's De-Luxe Mexican Dinner included a guacamole salad, chili con queso, a meat or cheese taco (the meat being ground beef), enchilada, tamale covered with chili con queso (also all beef), fried rice, fried beans, with toasted or plain tortillas. It also came with bread or crackers, a dessert and a choice of hot or iced tea, Coca-Cola or coffee, all for the grand sum of $1.75. The 1949 menu offers eggs on enchiladas, "spaghetti or rice con chicken," an appetizer of celery and olives, a three layer "Chef's Special Clubhouse" sandwich, pimento cheese sandwiches and a large selection of steaks, fried chicken, fried oysters, ham steaks and the "LIGHT-MEATY-TASTY Chilled Shrimp Plate" as well as fried White River catfish, lobster and peach halves stuffed with cottage cheese. It even served breakfast. Browning's, after all, wasn't just a Mexican-esque restaurant; it celebrated Arkansas foods as well and threw in the kitchen sink for good measure.

And yes, even on that first menu, there's the Plato de Saltillo, the dish the restaurant would be best known for, a meat taco and cheese taco and enchilada, smothered in cheese and served with tortilla chips. Back then, it was only a buck.

As the years went by, the restaurant expanded to other locations - on Baseline Road in Little Rock, on McCain in North Little Rock, even on the "New Benton Highway." Do you even recall the New Benton Highway? There was also El Patio on University, a spin-off that sold pureed "salsa" sauce with yellow chips in a bag that would always develop grease spots.

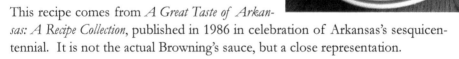

For a city and even a state that remained secluded and mysterious to the rest of the world, Browning's was a treat. Once the doors opened, and men like Sam Walton, Bill Clinton and the Stephenses managed to get Arkansas spoken of in terms that didn't include "hillbillies," things changed. Our palates changed. Browning's closed in 2010, only to be purchased, renovated and reopened and eventually fail again. Today, the location houses Heights Taco and Tamale Company, which honors the memory of Browning's with its Plato de 1947, its own version of the Saltillo Plate.

This recipe comes from *A Great Taste of Arkansas: A Recipe Collection*, published in 1986 in celebration of Arkansas's sesquicentennial. It is not the actual Browning's sauce, but a close representation.

Browning's Hot Sauce

2 #10 cans tomato paste
2 #10 cans crushed tomatoes
1 #10 can jalapeño peppers
1 cup chili powder
2 cups paprika

2 cups sugar
3 Tablespoons salt
½ Tablespoon garlic granules
1 Tablespoon cumin

Blend all ingredients in blender. Bottle and refrigerate.

ARKANSAW HOG SAUCE

The award winning Popa sauce is best known for its application on a pile of pulled pork on a hot dog bun. Ray Sisco came up with the sauce to go with what he'd grill. The grandchildren he and his wife Kathy spend time with gave the sauce its name.

ARMADILLO EGGS

These sausage- or bacon-wrapped cheese-filled jalapeño peppers are a tasty appetizer that appears on the menu at places such as Main Street Pizza in El Dorado. Combine biscuit mix, sausage and half the Cheddar cheese. Slice jalapeños in half, remove ribs and seeds. Blend together cream cheese and remaining Cheddar (include jalapeño seeds if you like spicy food).

1 cup biscuit mix
1 pound hot breakfast sausage
3-6 whole jalapeños
1 package pork flavor Shake N' Bake

8 ounces cream cheese
8 ounces shredded Cheddar cheese
3-6 slices bacon (optional)

Stuff jalapeño halves with cream cheese mixture. Wrap stuffed jalapeños, forming an egg shape. Shake eggs in Shake N' Bake until completely coated. Wrap in bacon and secure with a toothpick, if desired.

Bake at 350 degrees for 30 minutes to an hour (depending on the size of the jalapeños) until the sausage is cooked through. Or grill for 30 minutes, turning every 10 minutes.

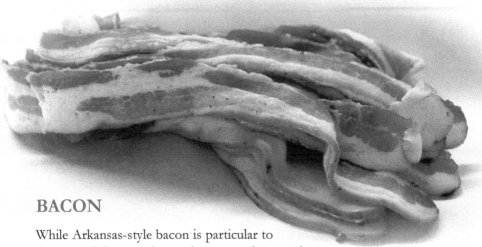

BACON

While Arkansas-style bacon is particular to
the state, Arkansas's largest bacon producer makes
its bacon the traditional way - from pork belly. Petit Jean Meats does a fine job
with its hickory-smoked bacon.

Coursey's Smoked Meats takes Petit Jean bacon and smokes it *again* for a double-smoked flavor. Old favorites like House of Webster and newer places like Bentonville Butcher and Pint offer everything from country smoked styles to lamb and beef bacon varieties.

Pulled pork plate at
Hoot's BBQ in McGehee.

BARBECUE

Arkansas lost one of its original meats -- goat -- thanks to changing tastes after World War II. However, the state has never been tied to one particular barbecue meat over another. There are mentions of barbecue in Arkansas all the way back to a Fourth of July shindig in Phillips County in 1821. The meats for political barbecues, themselves a culinary tradition dating back to 1840, were often whatever animals were donated by a community, whether beef or pork, chicken or turkey, venison or sheep or squirrel. The original tradition of barbecue in Arkansas came from the pit -- as in a long trough dug into the ground, filled with wood and lit aflame. The smoke from the embers would slowly flavor and cook the meat over hours. Over the generations, restaurant barbecue has been constrained, and at most Arkansas barbecue restaurants pork, beef and chicken are the available meats (with an emphasis on pork in the northeast, beef in the southwest and any combination with chicken in the northwest). The one influence Arkansas is blessed with retaining over all barbecue is its chosen condiment, coleslaw.

Beef brisket and corn on the cob at Blacksheep Joe's BBQ in Yellville..

Arkansas's only James Beard Foundation award winner is Mr. Harold Jones, who has worked at the family's restaurant in Marianna since 1964. The restaurant, a continuation of the former Hole In The Wall Diner once situated downtown, dates back more than a century, with the recipe for the thin vinegary sauce from just after the Civil War. Today at Jones Barbecue Diner in Marianna, you can have your pork in a sandwich "wi' or wi'out" slaw on white Sunbeam bread or by the pound – and that's it.

The Boyer family opened Central Arkansas's longest running barbecue joint, the White Pig Inn, in 1920. The Seatons purchased it in 1940, and today Greg Seaton is its owner. White Pig's claim to fame is its ribs, still hickory smoked with no timer or rotisserie, just smoke and heat.

Hot Springs is home to two of the state's best known barbecue joints. One was started by the family that ran the Westside Tourist Court, a motorcourt motel serving the needs of travelers coming to Hot Springs for the healing waters and the ponies. Back in 1928, there was one particular traveler who overstayed the contents of his wallet – and when he went to check out after two months, he didn't have the $10 he owed on the bill. So he made an offer -- for a barbecue sauce recipe he said was the "best barbecue sauce in the world," in exchange for his debt. The deal was struck, and soon the Westside Tourist Court became West-side Barbecue.

It wasn't long before Alex and Gladys Mc-Clard had themselves a winner. They re-named the shop under the family name. Folks came from all over to enjoy that sauce slathered on smoked goat. Pork and beef are the mainstays today (with smoked chicken on Wednesday). The most popular dish is Ribs and Fries, a slab of ribs served under a pile of French fries.

The other operation kicked up in 1952, when Richard Stubblefield Sr. started slow smoking pork, beef and chicken over fragrant wood om Park Avenue. He was a master of the hickory pit, smoking ham and ribs, pork butts, briskets and whole chickens. The sauce conjured at the restaurant was sweet, thick and mild. Stubblefield sold out to the Dunkels, a family who'd moved to Hot Springs from New York, in 1977. The Dunkels opened a second location in 1978 along Central Avenue just south of Oaklawn Park -- which remains the restaurant's key location. Susan Dunkel is still involved in the operation today, but it's her son Christopher's shop now. Outside of the excellent barbecue, one should try out the restaurant's Pot-O-Beans (*see also* Pot-O-Beans).

In Blytheville, the original Dixie Pig began in 1923. It sells "old-fashioned Southern pit sandwiches" with vinegar slaw. The Halsell family trace their lineage back to Ernest Halsell, the proprietor of the Rustic Inn, a log cabin that sat beside US Highway 61 and served "foods you like," as the sign out front said. The Halsells don't use spice or rub on those pork butts. Instead, they're seasoned only with smoke from charcoal and hickory until they fall apart. The sandwiches are a pile of meat and cabbage slaw on a bun. The sauce is thin, peppery and hotter than you think it will be. The combination is addictive. *See also* Pigmeat Sandwiches.

Lawrence Craig perfected his unique barbecue sauce while working a drag boat on the Mississippi. In 1947, he started offering that sauce on meat at a joint he opened with his brothers Leslie and Wes. Since then, the scent of Craig Brothers Café has wafted miles around DeValls Bluff, luring in the hungry for long-smoked pork hams, ribs, sliced beef, chicken and sausages.

Established in 1937, some would argue Sim's Barbecue as the particular flavor one should consider when thinking about barbecue in Little Rock. Known for fall-apart pork butt, pork ribs and beef brisket, it's the thin and tangy sweet vinegar sauce that makes this mainstay so memorable. Consider the barbecue bologna, and try a slice of sweet potato pie while you're there. *See* Barbecue Bologna.

Dozens of other barbecue joints around the state are worthy of note: Lindsey's Hospitality House in North Little Rock, H.B.'s Barbecue in Little Rock, Hall's BBQ in Dumas, Old Post BBQ in Russellville, The Backyard Bar-B-Q Company in Magnolia, Rivertowne BBQ in Ozark, Hoot's BBQ in McGehee and the Whole Hog Café chain (which started in Little Rock) all come to mind. However, sheer limitations of space call for making even this amount of barbecue talk brief

Half a smoked chicken at Old
Post BBQ in Russellville.

Two of the most notable sauces come from now-defunct establishments that made their own mark on Arkansas barbecue.

Wayne Shadden was the proprietor of his own business inside an old general store, a place that bore the name Shadden's Bar-B-Q. It has been oft reported that the place started out as a combination of barbecue joint and gambling hall. A $500 fine and a year in jail convinced him to just concentrate on the 'cue, which suited those who stopped in. The mild sauce was spicy, the hot nigh on unbearable and all of it meant to be consumed with an ice cold beer. Shadden closed the restaurant for the day in May 2010. He went home and passed away; the doors never opened again. Arkansas food lovers lamented. But we still have this recipe for the sauce, which was Wayne's wife Vivian's contribution to the two-handed sandwiches.

Shadden's Barbecue Sauce

1/4 cup oil
1/2 stick butter
2 small onions (chopped very fine)
3 Tablespoons Worcestershire sauce
3 1/2 bottle A-1 Sauce
3/4 bottle ketchup
11 Tablespoon chili powder

2 Tablespoons brown sugar
1/2 Tablespoon Tabasco
1/4 lemon (grated; including rind)
Salt and pepper to taste
Cayenne pepper to taste
  (for added heat)

Sauté onion in butter and oil until tender. Add other ingredients, mix well and cook for 30-45 minutes.

Grav Weldon

All central Arkansas barbecue sauce is measured against the memory of The Shack. Casey Slaughter's shop was a Little Rock mainstay from 1935 until its demise in the 1980s. Many restaurants claim lineage - the greatest among them H.B.'s Barbecue on Lancaster, not far from where I grew up, where Casey's brother Herbert Bruce Slaughter set up shop. Others who make the claim are Conway-based Smitty's Barbecue, Smoke Shack BBQ in Maumelle and the newest, situated in Little Rock's River Market District, also named The Shack. This version of the legendary sauce comes from Jim Cathcart.

Shack Sauce

4 cups ketchup
3 1/2 cups vinegar
6 Tablespoons chili powder
6 Tablespoons salt
6 Tablespoons sugar
6 Tablespoons black pepper
1 large onion chopped very fine

Mix all ingredients and boil slowly until thick, about three hours.

The Shack's sauce is so beloved, lots of folks have tried to duplicate it over the years. This recipe appears in *Happy Times with Home Cooking* by the Arkansas Grand Assembly of the International Order of the Rainbow for Girls (1990).

"THE SHOCK BARBECUE SAUCE"

Betty Jo Schrade
Adoniram #9

4 c. catsup
4 c. vinegar
4 c. water

6 Tbsp. black pepper
6 Tbsp. sugar
6 Tbsp. chili powder

Simmer slowly for 3 hours.
Keeps indefinitely in the refrigerator.

BARBECUE BOLOGNA

For a state that loves fried bologna and smoked meats, the combination of the two is inevitable. A number of Arkansas's barbecue purveyors offer slices of bologna from loaves smoked in the pit as an option for sandwiches. Some are served with barbecue sauce - like the bun-and-coleslaw version from Sim's Barbecue in Little Rock. Others, like that at Kibb's BBQ in Pine Bluff, serve it straight up, sometimes dressed with mayonnaise and lettuce.

BAR FOOD

It may seem a bit odd, but two of Arkansas's oldest dining establishments are, essentially, bars. That includes the oldest bar in the state, and the oldest restaurant in the state.

The Ohio Club along Central Avenue, across from the famed Hot Springs Bathhouse Row, opened in 1905. It started off as a nightclub and gambling house, eventually evolving into an eatery, which is why it's considered Arkansas's oldest bar but not its oldest restaurant.

John Coffee Williams and Sam Watt, his nephew, started the joint and named it after where they were from. Well, sorta. Williams had family in Kentucky and Illinois and Ohio, all three, but there was already a Kentucky Club and an Illinois Club, so The Ohio Club it was. Gambling was big in those days, and it was certainly taking place in Messrs. Williams and Watt's hall. The forbiddance of gambling in 1913 didn't slow things down, nor did the prohibition of alcohol in 1919. It drew famous performers, including Al Jolson, Mae West, Sammy Davis Jr. and Tony Bennett. Crime family members like Bugsy Siegel, Frank Costello, Bugs Moran, Lucky Luciano and Al Capone darkened the door. Early on, Teddy Roosevelt reportedly stopped in while president. Much later Bill Clinton, who grew up in Hot Springs, was a guest. Even after gaming became illegal, there were still games of chance going on in The Ohio Club, up to 1967.

Today, there's no gaming at The Ohio Club, but there's live music, the original 1880s barback and the best burgers in Hot Springs.

The oldest restaurant in the state, the White House Café in Camden, has an unusually styled custom made steel bar within. Hristos Hodjopulas, who had moved to southern Arkansas from Greece, opened it in 1907. The wedge-shaped edifice was built next to the train tracks, a two story chunk at the end of the downtown district, sharing space in the building with a grocery store. Shortly thereafter, Hodjopulas sold the place to his cousin James Andritsos, who kept it open 24 hours a day, seven days a week. The menu featured Kansas City-style steaks. Andritsos later sold the White House to a couple from China, Lum and Josephine Ying, who added chicken fried steak, meatloaf and hamburgers to the menu. Over the years nachos, enchiladas and fajitas were added to the offerings.

Today, the White House Café still stands, a whitewashed wedge spread across half a block on the east side of Adams Avenue. Plate lunches vary between roast beef, chicken and dumplings, chicken fried steak, meatloaf, smothered pork chops, and there's always fish on Fridays. The side dishes listed each day could come from any Lower Arkansas home – candy yams, fried potatoes, cabbage (sautéed in a pan), turnip greens, pinto beans, squash, PurpleHull peas or buttered corn or whatever happens to be available that day. A slice of Texas toast or a johnny cake comes along with the plate, and there's usually a slice of icebox pie, a scoop of cobbler or a chunk of pound cake for dessert.

BASS

A delicious sporting fish which can be prepared a number of ways. Bass fishing is quite popular in Arkansas. Largemouth bass are common in all of the larger lakes, while smallmouth can be found in rivers such as the Saline, the Caddo and the Cossatot. The nation's largest bass boat manufacturer, Ranger Boats, is in Flippin.

BEAN DIP

Primarily a side component at The Cow Pen in Lake Village, bean dip or refried beans are also featured across the state at various Ark-Mex, Tex-Mex and Mexican restaurants.

Floyd Owens bought an old station back in 1967 and turned it The Cow Pen. He started the restaurant to serve the folks coming across the old Benjamin G. Humphries Bridge from Greenville. Ten years later he turned it over to Gene and Juanita Grassi, who would run it for thirty years. They served a mean steak… and they added some other ideas too, ranging from catfish to Mexican fare to the Italian dishes popular in the area.

The Grassis decided to retire in 2007, and handed the reigns over to Charles Faulk and his family. Sadly, six months later the place burned down. That didn't deter the Faulks, who dove into the task of rebuilding it bigger and better. And since reopening in November 2008, The Cow Pen has flourished.

BEAN POT

During the winter months, it is not uncommon to see a big pot of beans kept on the back of the stove. Beans that are dried after summer's harvest are cooked up and allowed to sit and "mature," often with an added meat element such as bacon, ham or smoked turkey. The slow, long simmer usually reduces the beans and additives into a thick, protein-packed soup.

The Monte Ne Inn Chicken Restaurant offers a bean pot alongside the rest of the fixins that come along with its famed fried chicken dinner.

BEANS AND HAM

Similar and sometimes concurrent with bean pot, beans and ham are a particular delicacy enjoyed across the state, particularly with a slab of cornbread. The beans vary to what's available at the time - navy beans, red beans, pinto beans and brown beans are all acceptable. The beans are simmered for hours together; a ham bone; chopped ham, sliced onions and celery are all acceptable additions to the pot.

BEEF

Northwest and north central Arkansas and the Arkansas River Valley are home to dozens of family-owned beef and dairy cattle farms. The Ozark plateau and Arkansas's four-season year provide a great place for bovine production.

Sixty head of cattle were listed amongst livestock at Arkansas Post in 1749. Cattle were brought to Arkansas by early Anglo-American settlers and Cherokee families who moved into the state in the 1780s. They were key to subsistence farming in the Ozarks. Arkansas was a starting point for the cattle drives sparked by the California Gold Rush in the early part of the 19th century, and by 1860 there were 567,799 head of cattle in the state. But the Civil War decimated that population. Drives of cattle, predominantly Texas longhorn, pushed through northern Arkansas after the War as Texas ranchers drove the beasts to yards in Chicago, earning the ire of local farmers and Native Americans settled there.

Today, beef cattle can be found in every one of Arkansas's 75 counties – but the population is centered in northwestern Arkansas, where the Ozark plateau offers verdant and lush grounds for grazing. The University of Arkansas Cooperative Extension Service estimates approximately 30,000 beef cattle farms in the state. In contrast to the poultry industry, ninety-seven percent of these farms are family owned and operated. Arkansas is primarily a cow-calf state, where producers largely raise calves for sale to buyers who then grow them until they are ready to enter a feedlot for later slaughter.

See also Steak, Corned Beef Sandwiches *and* Burgers.

BEER

Up until the past few years beermaking in Arkansas was limited to a handful of microbreweries and one commercial brewery, Diamond Bear Brewery. A change in state law in 2014 allowed craft breweries to sell their products in growlers rather than just cans or bottles at any store with a beer permit. The craft beer industry began to boom. At the time of this writing, more than two dozen craft breweries are in operation in Arkansas.

Of these, Diamond Bear Brewery distributes in cans and bottles around the state, with several varietals and a non-alcoholic root beer. In 2014 Lost Forty Brewing came online, offering a selection of seasonal beers, ales and stouts in cans for retail and a restaurant at its brewery located in new and reclaimed developments on Little Rock's east side, near Heifer International's headquarters.

In 2013, an initiative to link northwest Arkansas breweries together began. The Fayetteville Ale Trail today connects ten breweries in the area via a passport program, and a van service is offered to take visitors to each one on a tour for a fee. Central Arkansas responded with its own program, Locally Labeled, in 2015 that connects the area's breweries, distillery and winemaking operations with a similar passport opportunity.

In Hot Springs National Park, Superior Bathhouse produces beer and distilled spirits directly from the thermal waters from the legendary springs. It's also the only operation producing beer in a national park.

BISCUITS

A staple of every Arkansas breakfast, ranging from medium-sized buttermilk biscuits to sweet biscuits that come within inches of being scones, to the cathead biscuit. The largest biscuits in the state are at Meacham's Family Restaurant in Ash Flat.

I have found this particular Angel Biscuit recipe in several different cookbooks, including the American Cancer Society's *Sampling Arkansas* Cookbook (1983) and *Recipes, Legends, and Such of Pickles Gap, Skunk Hollow and Toad Suck* (year unknown) - the latter of which was submitted by Helen Nunn.

Angel Biscuits

5 cups all-purpose or bread flour	2 cups buttermilk
¼ cup sugar	1 cup shortening or butter
3 teaspoons baking powder	2 Tablespoons lukewarm water
1 teaspoon baking soda	1 package active dry yeast
¼ teaspoon salt	Melted butter

Combine the first five ingredients in a large bowl. Make a well in the center and stir in shortening or butter and buttermilk. Dissolve yeast in lukewarm water and stir into mixture. Mix well. Roll out onto floured surface. Cut with biscuit cutter and dip in melted butter. Place on baking sheet, cover and let rise 30 minutes. Bake at 400 degrees for 15 minutes or until browned.

BISCUIT PUDDING

A recipe reportedly handed down from Liberty Bell, the proprietor of a classic restaurant bearing her name in Forrest City and now the specialty at an eatery run by her descendants, the Ole Sawmill Cafe.

Biscuit Pudding For Supper

5 eggs
3 cups sugar
2 teaspoons vanilla
4 cups whole milk
½ cup (1 stick) butter

1½ cans (total of 18 ounces) evaporated milk
¼ teaspoon nutmeg
¼ teaspoon cinnamon
1- 9"x11" pan leftover buttermilk biscuits or equivalent

Combine all ingredients and place in baking dish; cover with biscuits. Bake for 18 to 20 minutes at 350 degrees. Do not overbake. Remove from oven while dish is still jiggly.

Sauce:

½ cup (1 stick) butter
½ cup sugar
1 teaspoon vanilla

1 Tablespoon heavy cornstarch
1 cup water

Simmer in saucepan until it thickens, then spoon over biscuit pudding.

BLACKAPPLES

The proclaimed king of Arkansas apples, the Arkansas-cultivated Blackapple (or Arkansas Black) has received recent appreciation from gourmet chefs coast-to-coast. They're hearty apples that last through most of the winter, with a firm but crisp texture, sweet with little tartness. They tend to be dark red in color, darkening to burgundy and almost black over the season except where direct sunlight does not reach, where they are more likely to be yellow. A cultivar from the mid-19th century, Arkansas Blackapples can be kept for six months. They are mild and best paired with a tart apple for piemaking.

Illustration by Amanda Almira Newton, held by the Department of Agriculture Pomological Watercolor Collection.

BLACKBERRIES

Indigenous to Arkansas, the druplet-clustered fruit is a popular addition to the summertime table in pies, jams and cobblers. The University of Arkansas has created several cultivars from these native berries that are now utilized worldwide, including thornless versions and primacanes — blackberry plants that produce the first year they're planted.

I cannot recall a time in my life where blackberry picking wasn't on my calendar. Even as a small child, I remember reaching up past the prickles (what most folks call thorns) into a bush and grasping juicy berries right off the vines. I also recall time scrubbing with lye soap, trying to get chiggers off.

The blackberry is an indigenous fruit for Arkansas. You may not realize it, but each little druplet is its own fruit, formed around its own pollinated center. That's something to consider as you slowly work your way through a roadside bramble, pulling and plunking those berries.

My mom says June 19th is the day blackberries are ready. It was her grandmother's birthday, and the family tradition had been to go out picking that day. There are always preparations to be made. No sandals or bare feet, thanks to the chiggers, ticks and potential snakes. No shorts. Blackberry picking means donning boots or tall sneakers with long socks, heavy duty jeans and long sleeves. Even the most careful picker is bound to get scratches, but bug spray all over and tucked-in pant legs at least minimizes the tick potential.

My friend Leif often invites us up to his family's land near Alread, where the blackberry vines climb bushes and trees to make a truly tangled mess. Around my mom's place in southern Faulkner County, the vines are wound around barbed-wire fences. Wherever I go, it's a matter of wading in… and after years of experience, I know how to get into a good spot where the deer haven't eaten the best berries by carefully pinning down outside vines with my foot while reaching in to pull five or six berries at a time through a small window of vinelets. I don't even worry about breaking the berries as they drop – they're pretty resilient. The sound of berries plopping into pots and buckets is just as much a sound of summer as the high pitched roar of cicadas or the creaking of toads and frogs at sundown.

It's harder work than it looks, usually conducted in the brightest sunlight. Hats are a good option, but be sure to check yours for ticks, since ticks fall from trees. Drink plenty of water, too, because you will sweat it out.

Blackberries don't require much washing, unless you've been picking along a road, and then it's best to let them sit in a colander under water for a few minutes to get the dust off. There are so many ways to eat them. Blackberry cobbler's the hands-down favorite, but there's also blackberry pie or ice cream. When I was much younger, all I needed was a little Eagle brand sweetened condensed milk and I was in heaven.

What's not eaten right away usually goes into jams or jellies. Grav puts up blackberry jelly from what we don't immediately eat, and a couple of gallons of berries will get us through the winter on toast, English muffins and biscuits.

Black-eyed Pea Salad at William's Tavern Restaurant at Historic Washington State Park.

BLACK-EYED PEA SALAD

Also called Arkansas Caviar, this is a cold salad of black-eyed peas, onions, bell pepper and other vegetables in a sweet vinegar sauce. It seems to enjoy popularity in Lower Arkansas. This recipe comes from the Allen Packing Company, which is best known for Popeye Spinach.

Black-eyed Pea Salad or Arkansas Caviar

1 can (15.5 ounce) Allen's Black-eyed Peas, drained
1 medium chopped onion
¾ cup chopped red bell pepper
¾ cup chopped green bell pepper
1 seeded jalapeño, seeded and minced (optional)
3 green onions, chopped
¼ cup minced fresh parsley
1 jar (2 ounce) minced pimento
1 garlic clove, minced
1 bottle (8 ounce) fat free Italian dressing

Combine all ingredients and toss gently. Cover and refrigerate for 24 hours.

BLACK WALNUTS

This variety of tree nut is indigenous to Arkansas. The outer hull has long been used for medicinal purposes, hair dye and ink. Its inner nutmeat is pliant and slightly savory.

If you ever visit Jasper, be sure to stop in at the Arkansas House. Janet Morgan's famed Black Walnut pie, originally served at the Boardwalk Café attached to the property, is a 100-mile all-organic pie with a definitive flavor.. Made with black walnuts and sorghum, it's definitely something you'll find yourself craving long after you've returned home. Here's the recipe.

Black Walnut Pie

1 unbaked 8-inch pie shell
1 cup black walnuts, chopped
1/4 cup butter, melted
1/2 cup brown rice syrup

1/2 cup sorghum molasses
3 eggs, beaten
1/2 teaspoon vanilla

Spread the chopped walnuts over the bottom of the pie shell and set aside. Blend the butter and syrups with the eggs and vanilla. Pour the mixture over the nuts in the pie shell.

Place the pie in a pre-heated 425 degree F oven for 15 minutes. Reduce the heat to 350 degrees F and continue baking for 25 minutes or until top cracks slightly. Cool thoroughly before cutting.

BLUEBERRIES

Native to North America, blueberries cultivate very well here in Arkansas, and several you-pick-em farms offer a chance to take home your own during the late spring.

The University of Arkansas Division of Agriculture says blueberries can be successfully grown in all parts of Arkansas. Highbush adapts well to the northern counties, since they require cooler nights and aren't as tolerant of heat in the summer. Rabbiteye or Southern highbush does better in Lower Arkansas. Both grow well in Central Arkansas.

Dozens of you-pick-it operations around Arkansas offer blueberries, including Wye Mountain Farms in western Pulaski County.

BRADLEY COUNTY PINK TOMATOES

An original Arkansas cultivar, this fruit gets its name from its translucent skin through which the red heart of the tomato can be seen, giving it a light red or pink appearance. The thinner skin is also easier to bite into and through, and the fruit bears a strong, pleasant flavor.

The little town of Warren celebrates the county's famous fruit. The particular varietal is Arkansas's state fruit and vegetable, and in the late 1960s some 900 local farmers grew and sold the beauties. Thanks to competition from California and Mexico, just five or six farms around Warren still grow tomatoes in their fields today. The Bradley County Pink Tomato Festival is held each year the second weekend of June in downtown Warren. It includes the annual Tomato Feast, which you see below. Everything in the tomato feast has tomatoes in it - from the tomato crackers to the tomato carrots to the tomato beans and even the Heavenly Tomato Cake.

This recipe comes from Michelle Carter and Denisa Pennington, and was published in the handout for the Tomato Feast for the 2018 Bradley County Pink Tomato Festival in Warren.

Heavenly Tomato Cake

1/2 cup margarine
1 teaspoon soda
1/2 cup shortening
1/2 cup tomato juice
2 cups sugar
1 cup hot water

2 eggs
1 teaspoon vanilla
1/4 cup cocoa
1 1/2 cups miniature marshmallows
2 cups flour

Cream together margarine, shortening, and sugar. Add eggs one at a time beating well after each. Sift together cocoa, flour, and soda. Add to creamed mixture mixing thoroughly. Combine tomato juice, hot water and marshmallows; add to batter. Add vanilla. Batter will be thin and marshmallows will come to top. Pour into 15 1/2" x 10 1/2" x 1"jelly roll pan lined with parchment or wax paper. Bake in 350 degree, preheated oven for 35 minutes. Turn cake out onto a board.

Icing

1/2 cup margarine
1/4 cup tomato juice
2 Tablespoons water
4 Tablespoons cocoa

1/4 teaspoon salt
3 1/2 cups powdered sugar, sifted
1 cup chopped pecans (toasted)

Combine margarine, tomato juice, water, cocoa and salt; heat until boiling. Pour over powdered sugar and beat well. Add nuts and spread on hot cake. Ice cake while icing is hot.

Loaves on a shelf at Neighbor's Mill in Harrison.

BREAD

Man cannot live by bread alone, but when it comes to dining in Arkansas, bread is one of the most important things to come to the table. A restaurant is often recognized by the fine quality of the dough and crust, or how it is served. From the sesame seed encrusted loaves at Lazzari Italian Oven in Jonesboro to the butter-soaked loaves at Murry's Restaurant near Hazen, the soft pliant loaf for slicing at the Monte Ne Inn Chicken Restaurant near Rogers to the buttered slices at Dannie's Café near Hope, shared bread is so very much part of the dining experience.

Bread also comes to us from our master bakers. Of note is the famed Serenity Farms, operating for decades in Leslie; Neighbor's Mill in Harrison; and The Old Mill Bread and Flour Company in Little Rock.

Buttered bread at Murry's Restaurant in Hazen.

Crusty sesame seed studded loaf
at Lazzari Italian Oven
in Jonesboro.

Shared loaf of soft bread at Monte Ne Inn
Chicken Restaurant near Rogers.

Doughnut bread pudding at Wilson Café in Wilson.

BREAD PUDDING

A popular dish in New Orleans, bread pudding has been assimilated into Arkansas cuisine. Several versions exist today, including a traditional version served at Murry's near Hazen; one made from hamburger buns at the sadly departed Uncle John's in Crawfordsville; a chocolate version at Taylor's Steakhouse near Dumas and a version made from doughnuts at the Wilson Café in Wilson. This recipe came from the long gone Fayetteville Hilton.

Ozark Bread Pudding

1 quart cubed bread
1 Tablespoon butter
Cinnamon to taste
Raisins

1/3 cup sugar
1 egg
Vanilla to taste
1 cup milk

Scald milk, combine with egg, sugar and vanilla. Add raisins and cinnamon. Pour mixture over bread in a 1 ½ quart mold and bake in a water bath, covered, at 375 degrees. Bake for approximately one hour or until well set. Pour whiskey sauce over the top and serve.

Whiskey Sauce

2 egg yolks
2 Tablespoons sugar

¼ cup melted butter
Whiskey to taste

Beat yolks over moderate heat until thick and lemon colored. Remove from heat and gradually beat in butter. Add sugar and whiskey. Yields six servings.

BRITTLE

Once popular around the state, just a handful of brittlemakers remain. For years, Andrews Brittle Company and Juanita's Candy Company competed against each other with brittle in Arkadelphia, but Andrew's picked up and moved to Colorado in 2011, leaving Juanita's the state's brittle champ.

Juanita Smith started cooking brittles in 1974. She cooked up batches of peanut brittle in a small building located behind her home and then peddled her candies from her car around the state. One taste of that thin and crispy brittle was enough to get most folks to buy. Cashew and peanut brittle soon joined the lineup. Smith passed away in 2010, and her business passed into new hands in 2015. But those big white buckets of brittle are still a popular gift for newcomers.

BROWN BEANS

Another name for pinto beans, these legumes are often boiled together with bacon or ham for a simple, filling meal, often served with cornbread.

Brown beans at Shorty's
Restaurant in Providence.

BROWN GRAVY

A dinnertime staple, as opposed to cream gravy used at breakfast, brown gravy is made from roasted beef or venison drippings. It's a popular choice to top white rice as a side dish. Here's a simple recipe.

2 cups water	1/4 cup oil
Beef base or bullion cubes	1/2 cup flour
(enough to make two cups)	1/2 teaspoon black pepper

Dissolve beef bullion or beef base into the water; set aside. Whisk together flour and black pepper; set aside.

Place oil into sauce pan and heat on medium. Once oil is hot, add flour mixture and keep stirring with wire whisk until the mix is a blonde color. Add the beef/water mix, until desired thickness is reached and remove from heat. If not serving immediately, whisk again before serving.

Rice with brown gravy at
Franke's Cafeteria in Little Rock.

BROWN N' SERVE ROLLS

Created by Charles T. Meyer, Jr. of Meyer's Bakery on West Seventh Street in Little Rock in the 1930s, these rolls became the go-to dinnertime bread for generations of people all across the United States. The partially cooked rolls would be packaged in plastic and were shipped to grocery stores, where home cooks could take them home and refrigerate them until they were needed.

BRUNO'S LITTLE ITALY

The Bruno family ancestors purportedly cooked for the kings of Italy, mastering the authentic recipes of Italian cuisine handed down through the family. In the late 1900s, brothers Giovanni and Gennaro Bruno, new immigrants from Naples, opened one of the first pizzerias in New York City. Giovanni's son, Jimmy Bruno, began working in the pizzeria at age six. Jimmy was later drafted in World War II, where he served as chef of the mess hall at Camp Robinson in North Little Rock.

After the war, Jimmy moved to Chicago and opened the first pizzeria on Wabash Avenue on the city's famous Loop. After discovering the discouraging trend of organized crime taking over many legitimate businesses, Jimmy returned to Arkansas in 1947 and opened the Little Italy Café in Levy. It wasn't long before he outgrew the space and relocated to Roosevelt Road in Little Rock, changing the name to Bruno's Little Italy. The restaurant moved over the years, first to Old Forge Drive, then Bowman Road, then to Little Rock's Main Street in 2013.

Today, a clientele of both new customers and generational returnees frequent the eatery, still family-owned today. The same recipes utilized by Giovanni Sr. and Gennaro more than 100 years ago are still offered today - homemade marinara and meat sauces, lasagna, manicotti, ravioli, Italian sausage, cheesecake, cannoli, and the dish Brino's holds claim to introducing to Arkansas - pizza.

BUFFALO

Buffalo brisket at Big Spring Trading Company in St. Joe.

According to the *Encyclopedia of Arkansas*, undomesticated bison were present in Arkansas before the arrival of European explorers and settlers. Both the expedition of Hernando de Soto and the Marquette-Joliet expedition reported the presence of these animals.

Today, L.C. Ratchford raises buffalo and cattle on his family's 400-acre farm near Marshall. Ratchford has utilized his welding experience and scrap metal from the highway department and deep oil rigs to create a habitat suitable for raising the majestic, oversized animals. He utilizes nearby springs to provide the herds with clean, fresh spring water free of contaminants.

Buffalo products from Ratchford Farms are available at several grocery stores in the region. Burgers and steaks are served at the Boardwalk Café in Jasper and a few other restaurants. Buffalo summer sausages and snack sticks are available for purchase at stores throughout Arkansas.

Grav Weldon

BUFFALO (FISH)

Three different types of fish are considered buffalo in Arkansas – black buffalo, bigmouth buffalo and smallmouth buffalo. They all have the same nature when they come to the table – white flesh, veins of dark fat and oh so many bones. Because of this, most folks who enjoy buffalo dine on those ribs.

When I was a child and caught my first buffalo in the Saline River, I was given an option – catch it for bait or throw it back. We sliced meat right off the fish there in the boat and sank our hooks back in for more fishing, for catfish and whatever else might be lurking. Because of this, buffalo ribs were an experience I encountered first as an adult, unprepared at a fry where I was almost alarmed by the flavor. I'd been expecting catfish or bass but buffalo's unique flavor opened my eyes.

You'll find buffalo more often in soul food kitchens than fancy restaurants. At the top of the list of places that carry the delicacy is the Lassis Inn. This little blue house off Roosevelt Road in Little Rock goes overlooked (indeed, many residents have no idea where it is and only know whispers of its mythical existence). But these past few years, as interest in true Southern and Arkansas foodways has stirred up, more individuals have made it up the steps and into the tight interior, where a sign overhead admonishes "No Dancing" to its patrons (there were incidents where sinks were busted up and broken).

Lassis Inn offers catfish fillets and steaks and the famed buffalo ribs, which come thin but long (five to six inches each) to the table. The bottom-feeder flavor is strong, but for those who decide they can take it, it's a treat. For the rest, there's the catfish, which is excellent, as are the hush puppies.

The Bull Burger at Smokin' Bull in Emerson.

BURGERS

Arkansas is blessed with more than its fair share of great burger joints... hundreds of drive in restaurants, dairy bars, pubs, greasy spoons and diners serve up hot beef patties on buns with all the accoutrements.

To include even a small number of the burgers offered in Arkansas would take a book. In short, burgers are a significant part of the casual culinary landscape in Arkansas.

The Big Orange Burger at Big Orange.

The Ohio Burger at The Ohio Club in Hot Springs

Arkansas's cheapest burger: the original hamburger at Rich's Burgers in Pine Bluff.

Shroom Swissalaka Burger at Feltner Brothers in Fayetteville.

Arkansas's spiciest burger: the Inferno Burger at Lewis Family Restaurant in Fort Smith

Arkansas's largest burger: the five pound cheeseburger at Ed Walker's Drive In in Fort Smith

BUTTER BEANS

A perennial Arkansas garden selection, these are the better looking cousin of the lima bean. They can be greenish and somewhat immature, mellow and lightly yellow or speckled with maturity. Along with PurpleHull peas, something I spent more than my fair share of time shelling as a child.

Southern Style Butter Beans

6 ounces salt pork, sliced
1 pound large lima beans

1 teaspoon salt
½ teaspoon fresh ground pepper

Rinse and drain beans. Put salt pork slices in the bottom of a large eight quart pot. Pour the beans on top. Cover the beans with about a half-inch of water. Bring to a slow boil and reduce the heat to simmer (do not boil or stir). Cover pot loosely. Check every 20 minutes to make sure water covers beans – add more if necessary.

Simmer for two to three hours. Remove and discard salt pork. Add salt and pepper and stir. Add more salt and pepper to adjust flavor.

BUTTER CAKE

A cousin to the St. Louis Gooey Butter Cake, this simpler version (also known as a quarter cake or cuppa cake) is made using nothing more than a cup of sugar, a cup of flour, a stick of butter and an egg. The spongy cake base could easily be augmented with the addition of fruit, a compote, a frosting or icing or even chocolate. One of the last purveyors of butter cake, Bonnie's in Watson, closed in 2014. This is not Truvy's "Cuppa Cuppa Cuppa Cake" from *Steel Magnolias*.

1 cup self-rising flour
1 cup sugar

1 stick butter
1 egg

Heat oven to 350 degrees. Grease 9" x 9" pan. Cream together sugar and butter. Add egg. Fold in flour. Turn out into pan. Bake at 350 degrees for 30 minutes or until toothpick comes out clean. Serve with fruit compote or freezer-sweet strawberries.

BUTTER ROLL

A popular dish in the Arkansas Delta, this is a marriage of the idea of cinnamon rolls in a pan and good, fresh, hot dinner rolls.

2 cups all-purpose flour	1/4 cup white sugar
1/2 teaspoon salt	1/2 teaspoon ground nutmeg
1 cup shortening	2 cups milk
1/2 cup water	2/3 cup white sugar
3/4 cup butter, softened	1 teaspoon vanilla extract

Preheat oven to 350 degrees F. Lightly grease a 9" x 12" baking pan.

In a large bowl, mix together flour and salt. Cut shortening in thoroughly with a pastry blender until mixture resembles breadcrumbs. Stir in water and press dough together with your hands. Roll out pastry into a large rectangle. Spread the butter evenly over the pastry, then sprinkle on 1/4 cup sugar and nutmeg. Roll up the dough jelly roll style and pinch to seal. Cut into 12 even slices. Place the rolls in the prepared pan.

In a small saucepan, heat milk, 2/3 cup sugar and vanilla until mixture begins to bubble. Pour milk mixture over rolls.

Bake in preheated oven until brown, about 30 to 40 minutes. Serve hot.

BUTTERED CRACKERS

Butter on crackers goes back as far as buttering bread. The custom of adding butter to manufactured crackers is noted as long as there have been manufactured crackers. The practice of buttering crackers in restaurants is believed to have come from the earliest American restaurants where crackers were sold; for highway eateries, the unannounced appetizer became a staple for those too hungry to wait for dinner to be served.

The tradition continues with older diners in rural areas. Watch for older men drinking coffee and buttering crackers in diners. Try it yourself, if you choose.

BUTTERMILK

Traditional buttermilk is the remainder of the liquid left behind after butter is churned out of cream. Cultured buttermilk is created when the butter is left in and the milk is allowed to ferment from a starter. Hiland Dairy offers the traditional version on store shelves around the state.

Cultured buttermilk can be found at Dogwood Hills Guest Farm in Harriet, where the product is created entirely on the farm. Fodder for cattle feed is grown in a converted shipping container hydroponically. The fodder is then fed to the dairy cows that live on-farm. Those cows are milked, then that milk is set to ferment under controlled conditions. Guests to the farm can enjoy the buttermilk in many of the dishes created for the facility's farm-to-table dinners and even by the glassful. The resultant buttermilk is extremely thick with its original cream, which makes for decadent, tangy enjoyment.

CATFISH

Belzoni, Mississippi may claim itself as the World Capitol of Catfish, but it's a standard on Arkansas dinner tables, thanks to our 9700 miles of rivers and streams and all those lakes that provide plenty of catfish habitat. Catch your own, or dine on the delicacy at great restaurants such as Uncle Dean's in Cabot and Catfish Hole in Alma. A Friday standard state-wide, notably served with slices of white onion, lemon and green pickle relish (*see* Green Pickle Relish), alongside a mess of hush puppies (*see* Hush Puppies), of course.

My folks will tell you, don't measure out stuff to make fried catfish. You just make it. Thusly, most recipes I received for this book came as instructions, not measurements.

Fried Catfish Fillets
Heather A. D. Mbaye

Cut fillets into long pieces, soak in buttermilk at least three hours (all day is better). Mix plain yellow cornmeal (NOT "self rising" or "cornmeal mix") with salt and pepper to taste. Remove fish from butter milk. Let it drip for a moment and roll in cornmeal. Set aside. Roll all the pieces while a small vat of oil heats to about 375. Roll a second time and drop straight in the hot fat.

Parker Family Catfish
Dawn Parker

Put the liver on the hook. No cork. So it goes straight to the bottom. Reel in your fish. Warm up the fryer to 350 degrees. Clean the fish. Mix the fish fry seasoning with some Tony's and shake the fish in it. Put them in the fryer basket to cook - when they float, they're done.

Grady Fish Fry

Catfish at JJ's Café
in Lake Village.

Fried Catfish
Beverly Sanders

2 cups yellow cornmeal
½ cup all-purpose flour
1 teaspoon salt
½ teaspoon ground black pepper
(Watkins if available)
1 teaspoon seasoning salt

Dash garlic powder
Dash cayenne pepper
Catfish fillets, no thicker than ½ inch,
  fresh caught
Peanut or canola oil

Fill a cast iron Dutch oven 2/3 full of peanut oil or Crisco canola oil. Rinse catfish fillets and drain with paper towels under and on top. Mix together all other ingredients in a ziptop bag.

Bring oil to high heat. One at a time, place a piece of catfish in the bag, shake, remove and place in hot oil. Continue until several pieces are frying. Do not crowd – crowding will cause breading to fall off. When fish turns golden brown and is done, the fillet will float. Remove with tongs and drain on flat paper towel lined tray. Fish should be white inside. If pinkish, it is not done.
DO NOT leave frying fish unattended!

If also cooking French fries and/or hush puppies, cook fish first, then fries, then hush puppies. Remember to remove from heat when done.

The Whippet Dairy Bar and
Restaurant in Prattsville.

A cathead biscuit at Cathead's Diner in Little Rock.

CATHEAD BISCUITS

A staple of many Arkansas breakfasts, this pastry's name comes from the size and shape of the finished product, rather than its ingredients. Cathead biscuits are traditionally flaky and slightly dense, and because of their size moist on the inside. This recipe is from Brian and Reagan Eisele at the Oark General Store in Oark.

Cathead Biscuits and Gravy

Biscuits
4 Tablespoons shortening
2 cups WR self-rising flour
Splash of buttermilk
1 stick butter, softened

Rib-Sticking Bacon Gravy
1 to 1½ cups bacon grease
1 cup all purpose flour
1 Tablespoon salt
1 Tablespoon pepper
½ to 1 gallon whole milk

Preheat oven to between 400 and 425 degrees.

In mixing bowl, cut shortening into flour. Add buttermilk and mix thoroughly until dough reaches desired consistency. If dough is too sticky to work, add more flour, a little at a time. If dough is too dry, add buttermilk.

Grease a baking pan and then lightly coat the top of dough with flour—this will help keep your hands from sticking to the dough. Use your hands to softly press the flour into dough.

With a utensil roughly the size of a standard wooden spoon, scoop out a ball of dough and work gently with your hands to smooth it out. Place balls of dough onto greased pan until dough is gone.

With a pastry brush or paintbrush, spread softened butter on tops of biscuits. Then place the baking sheet in preheated oven for about 25 to 35 minutes, or until golden brown on top. Halfway through baking, repeat spreading butter on tops of biscuits.

When biscuits are desired color and size, take out of oven and spread butter over tops one more time. The biscuits should soak in the butter at this point.

In an iron skillet, heat bacon grease to medium-high on stovetop. Mix in salt and pepper with grease. When grease gets hot enough to make the flour sizzle, add in all-purpose flour while stirring constantly, eliminating clumps. The roux needs to reach a creamy consistency. If roux is too runny, add more flour a little at a time. If roux is too dry, add more bacon grease in same fashion. It's important to keep an eye on the flour, as it browns quickly. Use your nose to determine when the browning starts (we think it smells like popcorn), and mix in your milk once the flour is good and browned.

Remember to stir constantly. Turn heat down to a high simmer and reduce your gravy to desired consistency. You can always add more milk later to thin the gravy, if needed.

The Oark General Store is the oldest general store in Arkansas. Opened in 1890, it has remained in continuous operation, serving a community far separated from much of the rest of the state, not far off the banks of the Mulberry River. The restaurant within, opened in 2012 by Brian and Reagan Eisele, serves hamburgers, plate lunch specials and slices of pie along with generous breakfasts. While there's no cell signal in the area, the Oark General Store does have open WiFi, perfect for catching up between stretches of motorcycling Arkansas Highways 103 and 215 or kayaking the Mulberry.

CAVENDER'S GREEK SEASONING

Spike Cavender's commercial Greek seasoning is the secret ingredient for many Arkansas delicacies, especially burgers and steaks. The headquarters are located in Harrison.

Back in the late 1960s, Spike Cavender had a friend in the restaurant business who was dying, pass this specific spice recipe along. Cavender took that recipe and made it up with a friend from Oklahoma -- not to sell, but to give away to friends. It turned out to be rather popular, so in 1971, Spike and his son Stephen created the S-C Seasoning Company, and Spike's Greek Seasoning was born. Due to a trademark issue, the name of the company had to be changed, and thus today we enjoy Cavender's Greek Seasoning.

Cara Cavender Wohlgemuth and her sister Lisa Cavender Price run the company, along with their husbands and several longtime employees, and their mom Jane handles the mail-order business.

Thirteen spices go into Cavender's blend, but the proportions are a family secret. It's shelf-stable and will last a long time (though it may lose a little potency). There's also a low sodium version. The blend can be found in stores not only in Arkansas but across much of the U.S.

A wheel of Kent Walker Artisan Cheese; below, the cheeseboard at Nexus Coffee and Creative in Little Rock's River Market District.

CHEESE

While a few Arkansas dairies have offered small-batch cheeses, the introduction of the Raw Milk Bill in 2012 changed the cheesemaking game in The Natural State. Kent Walker Artisan Cheese became the first entry in the Little Rock market to start offering boutique, handmade cheeses in 2011. Walker's parents are winemakers; the experience he earned in that field prepared him for taking on this effort. In 2017, Walker sold the operation to Margie Raimondo, who incorporated cheesemaking into the fare served at her signature shared-bites restaurant in Little Rock, Southern Table. There, cheeses are paired with her wines and local meats.

Jessica Keahey opened Sweet Freedom Cheese in Bentonville in 2013. Keahey, who has studied cheesemaking all over the world, operates the only independent, cut-to-order cheese shop and education center in Northwest Arkansas.

Cheese is a common shared appetizer at many of Arkansas's restaurants. Nexus Coffee and Creative in Little Rock's River Market District offers one of the best, a meal-worthy shareable of cheese, meats, peppers and nuts.

CHEESE DIP

This single item of food connects all corners of the state. Created by the Donnelly Family, originally credited to his restaurant Mexico Chiquito, cheese dip has become a Southern staple. The great Ark-Mex restaurants of fame, from Pancho's in West Memphis to Glasgow's in Bentonville, all carry their own odes to this marvelous emulsion for chips and fries. The simplest version marries Velveeta and Ro*Tel together. The recipes for more complex versions are hoarded away.

In 2011, attorney and budding filmmaker Nick Rogers produced a documentary, *In Queso Fever*, where he sought out the roots of cheese dip and provided evidence of its origins. In 2016, a fight broke out between Texas Senator Ted Cruz and Arkansas Senators John Boozman and Tom Cotton over which state deserved the credit; a taste test between Uncle Julio's of Dallas and Heights Taco and Tamale of Little Rock came out with Arkansas on top. Texas calls their cheese dip, queso.

Cheese dip is celebrated with the World Cheese Dip Championship, which takes place in central Arkansas each October. Since it is so hotly debated, one recipe would not do for this tome.

Juanita's / Blue Mesa Style Cheese Dip

Released right after the restaurant closed, posted to Facebook, shared by the *Arkansas Democrat-Gazette* and promptly discounted by several members of the original Blue Mesa team (who agree it's not the original), this recipe was offered by the last crew of Juanita's. Since it remains a trade secret, this version will have to suffice.

5 lbs. white cheese melt
1 1/2 quarts milk
15 oz. canned diced
   green peppers
8 oz. finely chopped onions
3 oz. white pepper
2 oz. finely chopped cilantro
2 Tablespoon finely diced
   jalapeños

The ingredients should be cooked in a double boiler (or Crock Pot) until melted through. Then add more milk and stir until it reaches the desired consistency.

This following recipe is as close as I've found to the original served at Mexico Chiquito. Several different versions appear in dozens of Arkansas cookbooks.

Chiquito Style Cheese Dip

1 stick of butter
4 Tablespoons flour
1 teaspoon paprika
1 teaspoon chili powder
1 teaspoon ground cumin
1 teaspoon garlic powder
1 teaspoon cayenne pepper

1 teaspoon hot pepper sauce
1/2 teaspoon dry mustard
1/4 teaspoon salt
2 cups whole milk
1 pound Kraft American cheese, cubed (NOT pasteurized process cheese)

Melt butter in a saucepan. Add flour and stir around until flour loses its raw taste, about 3 minutes. Add spices and pepper sauce, then milk, stirring constantly. Add cheese and continue stirring until the cheese is melted and completely incorporated into the emulsion. Remove from heat. Serve with tortilla chips.

Ro*Tel® Famous Queso Dip

Arkansas consumes more Ro*Tel than all other states combined. This make-at-home dip is the reason why.

1 can (10 oz.) Ro*Tel® Original Diced Tomatoes & Green Chilies, undrained
1 pkg (16 oz.) Velveeta®, cut into 1/2-inch cubes

Place both ingredients in medium saucepan. Cook over medium heat for five minutes or until Velveeta is meted completely. Serve with chips.

Grav Weldon

This recipe appears in the *St. James Family Cookbook* published by Christian Mothers Fellowship St. James United Methodist Church in Little Rock (1984) and was contributed by Derby Fiser.

Pancho's Style Cheese Dip

1 pound American cheese, grated
1 can Ro*Tel tomatoes
1 teaspoon black pepper

1 teaspoon garlic powder
1 teaspoon cumin

Combine all ingredients and cook in a double boiler until cheese melts (to cook in a microwave oven, cover dish and cook at full power for two minutes; rotate dish and stir; cook two more minutes.) Serve hot with Tostitos. Note: It may also be served cold, but add about 1/4 cup water during cooking to prevent cold dip from being too thick.

This version appears in *Our Favorite Recipes* from the Sheridan Band Boosters (1980s printing) and is attributed to Terri Thirion.

El Chico Style Cheese Dip

2 tomatoes
3/4 onion

4 fresh jalapeños
1 medium box Velveeta

Heat 1/2 cup Wesson oil very hot in pan. Add 1/2 cup flour and mix good. Cook until kind of brown; do not let stick. Keep stirring.

(Editor's note: Make a roux with 1/2 cup vegetable oil and 1/2 cup flour until it reaches the color of caramel)
Chop all up and add to first mixture. Mix very good until it gets thick and pasty, cook about 15 minutes. Stir constantly.

Add 1 3/4 cups water and mix very good, then add medium sized box of Velveeta cheese (cut in small pieces) and stir. The more you cook it, the better the flavor.

CHEESE FILLED HOT DOGS

The Finkbeiner Meat Packing Company of Little Rock first created a hot dog with cheese inserted into the middle in 1956, though whether it was Otto or Chris Finkbeiner or one of their employees that created the "cheese dog" is lost to time. Today, Petit Jean Meats sells a version that incorporates both cheese and bacon in its filling.

CHEESE STRAWS

In 1987, Janis Parham and her daughter Melanie started baking and selling little finger-sized cheese straws. The tiny snacks were a little spicy, and also hot sellers. That little business grew into J&M Foods, which today is known not only for cheese straws but a variety of cookies.

Cheese straws have been a popular homemade snack for decades in Arkansas. This recipe from Dee Gladden appeared in *Sampling Arkansas*, a cookbook put out by the American Cancer Society's state chapter in 1983.

Cheese Straws

20 ounces extra sharp Cheddar cheese	2 teaspoons salt
7 ounces sweet butter	1 3/4 teaspoons baking powder
2 cups flour, sifted	3/4 teaspoons cayenne pepper

Finely shred cheese and cream with butter until smooth in an electric mixer or food processor. Sift all dry ingredients together and add to cheese mixture, mixing until smooth. Chill dough a few hours or overnight. Shape chilled dough into straws by forcing through the largest disc of an electric meat grinder, cutting into three inch strips. An alternate method is to roll as for pie crust about 1/4 inch thick and cut into three-inch strips with a knife. Place on ungreased cookie sheet and bake at 400 degrees for seven to tenminutes. DO NOT BROWN; remove from cookie sheets and place on cooling racks. Cheese straws will be doughy, not crispy. This is the secret to good cheese straws: put into a tin and place in a gas oven - with only the pilot light - overnight. They will be crisp and delicious.

CHESS PIE

The name of this dessert is a bastardization of its real name, "just pie." When you're broke and have nothing more for filling... or if you're aching for the simplicity of earlier times, chess pie is for you.

This recipe comes from the University of Arkansas Library, attributed to Ruth Chastang in 1978.

1 unbaked 8-inch pie shell
3 large eggs
1 1/2 cups sugar
1 Tablespoon cornmeal

1 Tablespoon vinegar
1/2 cup butter, melted
1 Tablespoon vanilla

Beat eggs with fork until light; add sugar, cornmeal and vinegar. Stir to mix well but do not beat. Add cooled butter and vanilla; stir to mix well. Pour into pie shell. Bake at 350° for 60 to 65 minutes. Serves eight.

CHICKEN

Pan-fried, deep-fried or pressure-fried – in Arkansas, we love our fried chicken. Born of similar dishes brought to the south by both African and Scottish ancestors, the traditional fried chicken served as "Sunday's best" generations ago remains on the table as the crispy-crusted comfort food of the South.

Before this land was settled by immigrants, the cuisine of Native Americans was based on what was available. Settlers brought chickens with them to Arkansas, and a meal made from a yardbird was a high occasion. Europeans who came here were accustomed to having their chicken roasted or stewed—traditions that date back from Roman times. The Scots are believed to have brought the idea of frying chicken in fat to the United States and eventually into the Arkansas Delta in the 18th and 19th centuries.

African slaves brought to the South were sometimes allowed to keep chickens—which didn't take up much space—and they flour-breaded, paprika-popped and spice-saturated pieces of plucked poultry before putting it into the grease. Frying in grease was hotter and quicker than boiling, roasting or baking, shortening cooking times. The propensity for jointing and processing chicken, skin on, by dipping in flour, buttermilk and egg and dropping it into a hot skillet full of hot oil or lard took hold.

If you are lucky, there's someone in your family who loves you enough to fry you your own chicken. But we're a state (and by extension a nation) of folks who have less time than we'd like, and we tend to want our fried chicken provided by a reputable restaurateur. More often than not, I fall into the latter category, and have therefore had my fill of bird from the top and bottom, mountains to Delta and everywhere in-between in Arkansas.

Arkansas ranks second in the nation in broiler chicken production. Tyson Foods is the nation's largest marketer and processor of chicken, and it's based in Springdale. Hundreds of Arkansas farmers make their living off raising this staple. It's also a popular roadfood from the early days of road travel in the state, and continues its reign at places such as Myrtie Mae's in Eureka Springs and the Monte Ne Inn Chicken Restaurant.

This recipe is from my aunt, Beverly Sanders.

Fried Chicken Breasts

3 cups all-purpose flour
1 teaspoon salt
½ teaspoon ground black pepper
1 teaspoon seasoning salt

3 chicken breasts
3 eggs
¼ cup 2% milk
Canola oil

Bring one inch of canola oil to high heat in a skillet. Cut breasts into ½ inch wide strips. Beat together eggs and milk in one bowl. In a separate bowl, mix other ingredients. Dredge each chicken strip in egg mixture, let drain, then turn in flour mix (remember to keep one hand clean and one hand for handling chicken). Turn burner down after placing first strip in oil. Work quickly to ensure chicken pieces will finish cooking together. Check chicken and turn when it browns. When both sides are golden brown, remove to a paper towel lined platter. Be sure to turn burner off and remove from burner. Make chicken milk gravy with the drippings if you like.

Ozark Fried Chicken

2 quarts cold water
1/2 cup non-iodized salt
1 chicken, cut into 8 pieces
1 quart buttermilk

2 cups peanut or canola oil
1 cup all-purpose flour
2 Tablespoons cornstarch
salt and pepper to taste

Stir salt into cold water until dissolved. Place chicken parts in a glass bowl; add enough brine to cover completely. Cover with plastic wrap and refrigerate eight to 12 hours. Drain brined chicken and rinse out the bowl it was brined in.

Return chicken to bowl, cover with the buttermilk, cover and refrigerate for 12 hours. Drain chicken on a wire rack, discarding the buttermilk.

Heat oil to medium high (will pop when flicked with water).

Sift together flour, cornstarch, salt and pepper in a bowl. Dredge drained chicken pieces thoroughly in flour mixture, then shake slightly to remove excess flour.

Put chicken pieces, skin side down, into the heated fat. Keep pieces from touching in the pan. Fry in batches, if necessary.

Cook for eight to 10 minutes on each side, until the chicken is golden brown and cooked through. Drain thoroughly on a wire rack or on crumpled paper towels, and serve.

Fried chicken thighs at Penny's Place in Weiner.

Chicken spaghetti at the former Ed and Kay's in Benton.

CHICKEN SPAGHETTI

A common staple of the daily lunch rotation at many longstanding establishments, chicken spaghetti is the peak of comfort food. The combination of protein and carbs will settle anyone into their afternoon. Unlike fried chicken and spaghetti, this is a conglomerate dish with a cream based sauce. There are an extraordinary number of chicken spaghetti recipes, a goodly number of them made from short-cut items such as Velveeta and canned chicken. This version, submitted by Jean Bailey of Barling for *Favorite Recipes* by the Fort Smith Chapter 10 of the National Association of Women in Construction (1981), is from scratch.

Chicken Spaghetti

1 large hen or fryer	1 bell pepper
2 large onions	2 Tablespoons Worcestershire sauce
1 1/2 cup celery	dash hot sauce
3 buttons garlic	1 can mushroom soup
1 small can tomato paste	1 small can mushrooms
1 small can pimento	2 cups grated cheese
1 teaspoon chili seasoning	10 ounce box thin spaghetti

Cook hen until tender. De-bone and set aside meat. Mix onions, celery, garlic, bell pepper with some of the fat from the broth. Add a little butter if needed. Sauté for 10-15 minutes. Add three cups broth, tomato paste, mushroom soup, seasoning, pimentos and mushrooms. Cook slowly about 40 minutes. Add chicken. Cook spaghetti in broth or salted water, then add to pot of other ingredients. Heat long enough to warm noodles. Put cheese on top and heat until cheese melts.

CHILI

A popular communal dish, chili is a winter's meal made from any of a number of proteins. Pride is taken in who can make the best, especially at the State Chili Cookoff and at the annual Big Buck Classic at the Arkansas State Fairgrounds. Chili suppers are a common fundraiser and social activity as well. For a beanless variety, *see* Venison; this is my own version.

3 pounds ground chuck, browned and drained
1 28 ounce can crushed tomatoes
1 28 ounce can diced tomatoes
4 bell peppers, flame roasted, skinned and diced (various colors)
2 whole diced onions
3 cans kidney variety beans (light red, dark red, cannallini), drained
1 can black beans, drained
1 teaspoon white pepper
2 teaspoons salt
5 Tablespoons cumin
1 Tablespoon minced garlic
1 Tablespoon butter

Sauté peppers and onions in butter over medium heat until onions are translucent. Add garlic and sauté for another minute. Add meat, beans, and peppers and stir. Add both cans of tomatoes, cumin, and salt and stir. Reduce heat to low and let simmer for an hour or more.

CHOCOLATE

Though the confection wasn't created in Arkansas, it has been part of our culinary heritage for decades. The two oldest chocolate makers in the state both trace their lineage to Martin L. Greer, who started making candy on his family farm in 1924 to supplement the family's income. Greer was hired on at a Greek candy shop out of Texarkana. From there he apprenticed his way through Texas, learning his way from hard stick candy to chocolate.. He opened one chocolate shop, but had to close it because of sugar rationing during the second World War. After the war, he opened another.

In 1956, Greer moved his family from Fort Worth to the Fort Smith area, where he opened Stateline Confectionery - which eventually became Kopper Kettle Candies. By then, he had a family, and everyone worked in the shop he and his wife Betty ran.

Greer's older son, his namesake, went to the College of the Ozarks and returned to Van Buren to teach art at the local high school. Stuck with a limited budget, he directed his students in building parade floats, constructing puppets for shows and creating animated movies. The money raised went to purchasing all the equipment needed for the students. In 2000, Dr. Greer would open Martin Greer's Candies between Gateway and Eureka Springs, where today he, his wife Jeanette, and sons Uriah and Joshua still make candies in the old world tradition with recipes from the 19th century.

Another son, Tommy Greer, would step in after his dad passed in 1978 to keep the store running with his mom. Today, he and the third generation of Greers continue to operate Kopper Kettle Candies along US Highway 71 in Van Buren, along with a second store in Fort Smith.

In the last decade, several other chocolatiers have come forward to create new and delectable cocoa-laden delights. One of the first of these is Cocoa Bella Chocolates. Arkansas's first professional chocolatier, Carmen Portillo, makes a lovely array of chocolate truffles alongside a line of chocolate sauces and butters.

In Little Rock, Izard Chocolate offers sustainably sourced, high-end chocolate bars made from Fair Trade beans, paired with well-considered ingredients such as California almonds, Icelandic sea salt, organic sugar and Madagascar vanilla in its bean-to-fork operation.

Then there's KYYA Chocolate, which started in 2012, a small Springdale company that meticulously curates chocolates from hand-picked cacao beans sourced directly from farmers from many of the 85 cacao producing countries around the globe. The chocolate takes 72 hours to prepare single-origin bars, baking bars and cocoa powder, sauces and syrups.

I'd be remiss in not mentioning Markham and Fitz Chocolates, which shares space in the Brightwater School for Food complex in Bentonville. The operation not only creates bite sized chocolates and candy bars, but offers drinks, desserts, confections and superfoods celebrating the cacao bean, a splendid experience to enjoy and share in the restaurant's gorgeous sea-green and white social room.

Chocolate gravy on biscuits at Gadwall's Grill in North Little Rock.

CHOCOLATE GRAVY

A delicacy with roots back to the Spanish, derived in its present form by innovative cooks looking to create something sweet. Two different versions exist -- one with bacon grease that's made from a traditional roux, and another (more commercially popular) from flour, sugar and butter. Cindy Grisham wrote about the substance in her book *A Savory History of Arkansas Delta Food: Potlikker, Sop and Chocolate Gravy*. Great examples can be found at Calico County in Fort Smith and Gadwall's Grill in North Little Rock.

Chocolate Gravy

Chocolate gravy on a biscuit at Calico County in Fort Smith.

3 Tablespoons butter
6 Tablespoons sugar
2 Tablespoons all-purpose flour
3 Tablespoons cocoa
2 cups milk

Heat butter in a skillet over low heat. Mix in sugar, flour, and cocoa. Slowly pour one cup of milk into the skillet and whisk well to remove lumps. Whisk in remaining milk, stirring constantly, until mixture is thick, being careful not to scorch. Serve hot over biscuits.

CHOCOLATE ROLLS

Searcy County, Arkansas is the World Chocolate Roll Capital -- which is undoubtedly true, since it's the only place in the world you can find them. The chocolate roll has been made by families around Searcy County for decades. I can attest to this. My brother's grandmother, Shirley Diemer, made these crumbly concoctions in her kitchen and in the restaurant where she worked so many years, the Downtowner in nearby Marshall. I can remember that crusty, chocolate combination back to the age of ten. Shirley, as the rest of the Diemer clan, was from Leslie.

Today, passers-thru traveling US Highway 65 can pick up a chocolate roll or a dozen at Misty's Shell Station in Leslie, a local convenience store where fresh chocolate rolls and fried pies are sold every day. If you're in Marshall, the place to get your chocolate roll is the Kenda Drive-In. I kid you not, Kenda Dearing's fantastic 50-year-old drive in operates year-round and offers some of the cheapest, best movie popcorn and concessions you'll find anywhere. Chocolate rolls are on the counter and they're $2 a piece – and worth every bite.

The Searcy County Chocolate Roll Festival is held each March, but for now, get yourself by Misty's or the Kenda and try one. Here's a recipe.

Searcy County Chocolate Roll

Pastry:
1 c. flour
1/2 c. vegetable shortening
1/4 c. cold water
dash of salt

Filling:
3 Tablespoons cocoa powder
1/3 c. butter or margarine
1/3 c. sugar

Incorporate all pastry ingredients into a pie crust-like dough. Roll out. Cream together cocoa powder, sugar and butter and spread on surface of pie crust. Roll from one end, tucking in sides like you would a burrito. Bake at 350 degrees for 10 to 15 minutes or until golden and molten. Let cool 10 minutes before serving.

A cellophane-wrapped chocolate roll at the Kenda Drive-In Theater in Marshall. The Kenda has operated continuously, year-round since 1966.

CHOW-CHOW

The late Southern food historian John Egerton theorized that chow-chow origi-nated in the piquant sauces brought over by Chinese railroad workers in the 19th century. Though those ginger and citrus combinations are uncommon in tradi-tional Arkansas fare, the pickling of end-of-harvest vegetables with vinegar is so common that it's rare not to find it on the rural table. The once-humble melange is now making a resurgence in the 21st century dining scene, not just in country cafés but in urban favorites such as Little Rock's Cathead's Diner. The common ingredients in most versions of chow-chow are vinegar, mustard seed, salt and green tomatoes, with cabbage, onion, corn, okra and even hot peppers also used. The flavor is an essential addition to greens, beans and other things. This recipe by Frieda Roberts of Cross County appears in *Arkansas Farm Favorites*, compiled by the Arkansas Farm Bureau Federation Women's Committee (1981).

Chow-Chow

1 peck green tomatoes
8 large onions
10 green bell peppers
6 hot peppers
3 Tablespoons salt

1 quart vinegar
2 1/2 Tablespoons pickling spice
  (tied in a piece of cloth)
1 chopped cabbage (optional)

Chop tomatoes, onions, peppers and cabbage; cover with salt. Let stand several hours or overnight. Drain; add vinegar and spices. Boil until mixture turns clear green (about 30 minutes). Put in hot jars and seal. Process in boiling water bath five minutes.

Ferguson's Country Store and Restaurant in St. Joe.

CINNAMON ROLLS

Arkansas has a long roadfood history with cinnamon rolls. The pastries, made from relatively inexpensive foodstuffs, keep a while and can be stored without refrigeration. They're both a substantial breakfast with coffee and a perfect meal-ending treat for lunch and dinner.

The largest can be found at Burl's Smokehouse in Royal, where they come big as your head. The throwback country store makes theirs light on the cinnamon but heavy on the dough for these all-day snackers. The second largest are at Daisy's Lunchbox in Searcy, where you can take home an oversized round in its own tin and every lunch comes with a more reasonable sized roll, packed with an extraordinary amount of cinnamon. The third largest is in St. Joe at Ferguson's Country Store and Restaurant, where the saucer-sized rolls come with a full cup of poured-over icing, necessitating a fork and a big cup of coffee.

Other notable cinnamon rolls can be found at Old Mill Flour and Bakery in Little Rock, with its tight-wrapped Everlasting Gobstopper, an un-iced delight. In Fort Smtih, Calico County has served more than eight million of their un-frosted sugar-and-spice rolls to hungry diners before they dine. Nellie B's Bakery in Elkins lightly glazes theirs; and in Hot Springs, you can choose the glaze you like for your roll at Will's Cinnamon Shop on Central Avenue.

Daisy's Lunchbox in Searcy.

Burl's Country Smokehouse in Royal.

COFFEE

Arkansas has quite a few coffee roasters. While coffee itself isn't grown in Arkansas, several businesses have made a point to bring in beans from other countries and roast them here. The largest, Westrock Coffee, has spread nationwide in just a few years. The North Little Rock-based operation works directly with its growers in Rwanda and Tanzania to bring beans here for roasting. Several others have followed suit, including Onyx Coffee Lab in northwest Arkansas, which started as an effort to create the most perfect sweet, black coffee around and which has become well-known for its coffeeshops and microbatch brews. Leiva's Coffee in North Little Rock gets its beans from Guatemala and aims to end farmer exploitation there. Airship Coffee in Bentonville focuses on good beans and great roasting, and teaches how to roast and how to be an excellent barista. And of course, RoZark Hills Roasters in Rose Bud, which has been around longer than all these already mentioned, focuses on medium and deep brews.

Black coffee at
Prelude Breakfast Bar
in Fayetteville.

Coleslaw at Rub 'Em Tender BBQ in Lavaca.

COLESLAW

I'm not saying Arkansas created coleslaw. I'm not even saying we were the first to put it on barbecue sandwiches. But the Arkansas standard for barbecue is shredded or sliced pork or beef, sauce on the meat, coleslaw on top, on white bread.

This recipe is from my maternal grandmother, Mary Waldon.

Coleslaw for Freezing

1 medium head cabbage, shredded
1 teaspoon salt
1 carrot, grated
1 bell pepper, chopped
1 cup vinegar
¼ cup water
1 teaspoon whole mustard seed
2 cups sugar
1 teaspoon celery seed (optional)

Mix cabbage and salt. Let stand one hour. Squeeze out excess moisture. Add carrot and pepper.

Combine vinegar, water, seeds and sugar in saucepan and bring to a boil for one minute. Cool to lukewarm. Pour over vegetables. Pack in one quart containers and freeze until needed.

COLLARD GREENS

Brassica oleracea acephala, one of the oldest members of the cabbage group, was cultivated by the ancient Greeks and Romans before the birth of Christ. It was first mentioned in records here in America in 1669.

Collards are basically wild cabbages that don't form into heads. They're related to kale. They're resistant to frost, which makes them good for harvesting nearly year-round. For summer collards, you plant in the spring; for winter collards, seeds are planted mid- to late-summer. They're full of vitamins A and C. The leaves range from dark green to bluish green in color.

You harvest collards from the bottom leaves out. The bigger leaves are mature. If you're growing them yourself, it's best to just pick what you need and come back for more later. Some folks grow both collard greens and mustard greens so they can cook them together, which makes for a more rounded flavor profile. Mustard greens tend to have longer, slightly skinnier leaves that are lighter in color.

Unlike some other greens like poke salat, you can eat every part of the collard. Wash leaves well to remove bugs and dirt before you cook it. Cut out the center stalk unless you're boiling your greens – they're tough and they take a lot longer to cook. Collard greens are a little more bitter than turnip greens. I like a shake of cayenne garlic sauce on mine. Cornbread is the best companion you can have for this dish. Don't toss the vitamin-rich potlikker, either – keep that for sopping.

See also Potlikker.

COMPANY'S COMIN' PIE

The Cliff House Inn is a small restaurant and gift shop and bed and breakfast perched over what we call the Arkansas Grand Canyon. It lies south of Jasper on the side of Scenic Highway Seven. It was originally opened in 1967 and has seen its share of owners. In the 1980s, owners Bob and Francis McDaniel began offering a signature biscuit and a signature pie – the latter of which permanently put the restaurant on the map.

Current owner Becky McLaurin says Francis McDaniel tried a lot of pie recipes before she stuck with this one, a pineapple pie made on a meringue and saltine crust. She called it Company's Comin' Pie. The pie soon received a following.

In 1986, a tourism campaign with the slogan "Company's Comin', Let's Get Ready" was rolled out by the state, and the Cliff House Inn's pie was ready for the spotlight. And thus, the Company's Comin' Pie was named the pie of the Arkansas Sesquicentennial. This recipe is the official version from the Cliff House Inn.

Company's Comin' Pie

3 egg whites
1/2 teaspoon cream of tartar
1 cup sugar
18 soda crackers, finely crushed
1/2 cup chopped pecans

1 teaspoon vanilla
1/2 cup whipping cream
2 Tablespoons sugar
2 Tablespoons crushed pineapple
   or pineapple preserves

Beat egg whites until foamy. Add cream of tartar. Beat until very stiff and dry. Gradually add sugar. Fold in crackers and nuts. Add vanilla. Put in lightly greased pie pan and pull sides up to form crust. Bake 30 minutes at 300 degrees. Cool.

Whip cream with sugar until soft peaks form and sugar is dissolved. Fold in pineapple or preserves, smooth into the crust. Refrigerate until ready to serve.

COON

No, we don't really eat coon all the time. But if you're planning on running for political office in Arkansas, you have to attend the trial-by-fire known as the Gillett Coon Supper. It's just part of the prerequisites. Each January, hundreds turn out to rub elbows, see friends and have a taste of smoked raccoon at the Gillett Coon Supper.

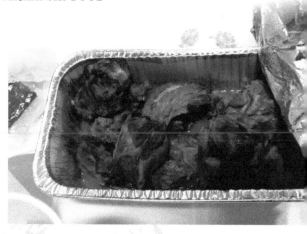

The wild animals are harvested by people in the community who set traps for the furry mammals. For a couple of months before the event, there's a stand alongside Arkansas Highway 1, where people turn them in. They're paid by the pound. The raccoon is cleaned, smoked and served up to the crowd in aluminum pans that are passed around the table.

Each year, 1200 tickets are offered, and it is always a sellout. You'll see all sorts of people from Gillett, but you'll also see politicians from all over Arkansas, and all over the United States. Somehow, this little shindig has become one of those famous political spots where the elite come to eat, shake hands and be seen. Barbecue pork and a variety of side items are also served family style at each table, and each place has a slice of cake on the side.

CORN

Sweet corn is a common accompaniment to the summertime table, still on the cob. Of the purveyors of the golden ears, you'll find none with as much fame as Esau sweet corn. It's the product of the farms of Chester and Carol Esau, a Mennonite couple who planted their first 20 acre crop of sweet corn near Dumas in 1990. Today, the couple along with their son Chad grow 160 acres of corn, which typically produces between mid-May and early October.

Creamed corn is popular any time of year, especially as a vegetable option for restaurant plate lunches. This recipe comes from the former restaurant Mama Max's, once a soul food staple in Prescott.

Mama Max's Creamed Corn

8 ears of corn shucked and washed	1/4 cup water
1 heaping Tablespoon flour	1/4 cup butter
1 heaping Tablespoon white sugar	salt and pepper to taste

Start by shucking and rinsing the corn so all the silk is removed. Trim the ends and cut kernels into a bowl. Scrape cob with back of knife to remove additional corn and juice from cob. Add flour, sugar and water. Mix well. Heat the butter on medium heat (or about 250 degrees in an electric skillet). Add corn mixture to pan and cook thoroughly until done (about five to seven minutes.) Salt and pepper to taste and don't forget to add the love.

CORNBREAD

Other states have cornbread, sure, but we love it so much, we have our own Cornbread Festival. We're also home to War Eagle Mill, which provides us both white (for non-sweet) and yellow (for sweet) organic cornmeal for our precious dinner bread.

Arkansas celebrates this golden substance each year with the Arkansas Cornbread Festival. Held along Main Street in Little Rock's SoMa District, it combines lots of fun activities with competitions between professionals and amateurs aiming to be named the purveyors of the state's best cornbread.

War Eagle Mill Cornbread

1 1/2 cups War Eagle Mill Yellow or White Cornmeal
3/4 cup War Eagle Mill All-Purpose Flour
2 1/2 teaspoons baking powder
1 Tablespoon honey or sugar

1 teaspoon salt
11/2 cups milk
1 egg
2 Tablespoon bacon drippings, butter, or vegetable oil

Preheat oven to 375 degrees. Add drippings or oil to an eight to ten inch cast iron skillet or nine inch baking pan and put in oven while it is preheating. In medium size bowl, stir together cornmeal, flour, baking powder and salt. Stir in milk, egg and honey or sugar. Remove skillet from oven and pour excess oil into batter. Mix well. Pour batter into hot skillet and return to oven. Bake 20- 25 minutes or until golden brown and firm.

For generations, the power of the War Eagle River has been harnessed to mill grain for the Ozarks. Farmers would bring bags of corn and wheat from their fields to War Eagle Mill to have the grain ground for bread and sustenance.

The mill dates back to 1832, when the first mill and dam were built by Sylvanus and Catherine Blackburn. The first mill washed away in a flood in 1848. The second, built on the foundation of the first, became the heart of a community with an attached sawmill and a blacksmith shop, church and school all on the same property. It was destroyed by Confederate troops, burned to the ground three days before the Battle of Pea Ridge in 1862. Sylvanus's son, James, built the third mill in 1873, but instead of using water power as his father had in the previous two mills, he used a steam-powered turbine to operate the machinery. It burned in 1924, and the foundation sat barren for nearly 50 years.

Jewell Medlin and his wife purchased a cabin on top of a hill that included the mill foundation in the deed. Jewell and his daughter, Zoe rebuilt and successfully reopened War Eagle Mill on that foundation in 1973. This fourth mill is powered by an undershot wheel, the only such device operating in all of Arkansas. Zoe and the man who would become her husband, Charlie Caywood, ran the mill for 30 years. They sold it in 2004 to Marty and Elise Roenigk of Eureka Springs.

War Eagle Mill continues to offer on-site ground organic grains and mixes, from cornmeal and flour to oats and grits, plus an array of fine jellies and jams. The mill is open every day during most of the year, and every weekend through the dormant winter months. In October, the massive War Eagle Craft Fair takes place across the river in the fields beyond. The Bean Palace on the third story of the structure offers sandwiches, cornbread, biscuits and pancakes made fom the organic, non-GMO grains ground on-site.

This version of cornbread, served at Dogwood Hills Guest Farm in Harriet, is gluten-free and especially rich with the house buttermilk.

Gluten-Free Buttermilk Cornbread

10-inch cast iron skillet, deep sided
2 Tablespoons shortening, butter
 or oil, melted in pan
1 1/2 cup yellow cornmeal
3 Tablespoons gluten-free flour
3/4 teaspoons salt

1/2 cup sugar (or to taste)
1 teaspoon baking powder
1 teaspoon baking soda
2 1/4 cup homemade buttermilk
2 farm fresh eggs

Preheat oven to 400° F. Mix all ingredients together and pour into hot skillet with the melted fat in it. Bake for 24 minutes until set and golden.

CORNBREAD IN SWEET MILK or BUTTERMILK

A common application practiced by generations of people in Arkansas and the South in general, sometimes enjoyed as a breakfast meal, sometimes a snack, and sometimes (with honey) as a dessert. Chunks of cornbread are placed in a glass and either milk (known as sweet milk over the ages) or buttermilk is poured over the top. The resulting mush is eaten like a warm cereal.

CORNED BEEF SANDWICHES

Introduced to Arkansas in 1904 at the opening of Oaklawn Racetrack in Hot Springs, Oaklawn's corned beef sandwich is the single oldest dish in Arkansas served consistently over the years from its originating point. The pickled meat comes in plastic barrels from the Kelly Eisenburg Company in Chicago. It's boiled in batches of around 150 pounds at a time in the kitchens beneath the park's public spaces.

It takes just a few seconds for the concessionaires at the park to assemble a corned beef sandwich. They're available with horseradish or with mayo, mustard or ketchup – and for a few dollars more, you can get a Reuben. They're available any time, but on the first Saturday of racing each January, that plain corned beef sandwich is just 50 cents.

That's the same price they were offered at when the track first opened. The sandwiches were served because many of the city's visitors came from the Chicago area, where corned beef was popular. Over time, the love for corned beef has spread across Arkansas, and you'll find it represented on a vast variety of menus here in Reuben sandwiches.

See also Reuben sandwich.

COTTON BLOSSOMS

A delicate appetizer offered with apricot brandy sauce, these cream cheese filled crisps are the go-to starter for meals served at Pine Bluff's famed Colonial Steak House.

COUNTRY FRIED STEAK

Well known as a Texas favorite, Arkansas eaters also love this battered and fried delicacy. The dish is usually served with gravy and a side of mashed potatoes. Beef is the usual meat used in this application; venison is also popular with families who hunt. Excellent versions can be found at Beech Street Bistro in Crossett, Taylor's Made Café near Mayflower, the Wagon Wheel Restaurant in Greenbrier and the Cliff House Inn near Jasper.

COY'S STEAK HOUSE SALAD DRESSING

A legendary restaurant that served Hot Springs for 65 years. The original Coy's Steak House was located in a log cabin at the corner of Central and Grand Avenues. Years later, a new location was built from the bricks of an old bank and constructed along US Highway 70 on the northeast corner of town. Famous for its steak seasoning, cheesecake, warm crackers and house dressing, longtime Arkansas food lovers were saddened in 2009 when the restaurant burned and the decision was made not to rebuild.

One of the most requested recipes I've been asked about over the years is this dressing. The original owner's son, Coy Theobalt, confirmed this recipe with me.

Coy's Steak House Dressing

1/2 cup vegetable oil
1 cup mayonnaise
1 Tablespoon paprika
1/4 teaspoon Accent seasoning
2 Tablespoons lemon juice, strained
2 Tablespoons white vinegar

1 Tablespoon garlic powder
  (not garlic salt)
1 Tablespoon sugar
1/4 teaspoon salt
1/2 cup evaporated milk

Blend all ingredients together. Refrigerate overnight. Serve on salad or saltine crackers.

*Coy Theobalt himself says NEVER serve it on Club crackers.

CRACKERS

See Pimento Cheese. *See also* Cheese Straws.

CRAFT BEER

See Beer.

CRAPPIE

Pronounced   CROP-ee,   one of the best-tasting gamefish you'll find any-where. Crappie isn't sold in restaurants -- it's against the law. But you can catch your fill at any of a number of Arkansas lakes and rivers.

Here's a recipe from the Arkansas Game and Fish Commission.

Savory Fried Crappie

6 crappie fillets
1 large lemon, cut in half
1 Tablespoon olive oil
1/2 teaspoon black pepper

1 egg, well beaten
1/2 teaspoon dry mustard
1 cup yellow cornmeal
Peanut oil for frying

Place fillets in a bowl and squeeze the lemon over the fish. Be sure each piece is thoroughly coated with juice. Pour olive oil over fish, add the black pepper and egg, and work into the fillets. Add the dry mustard, and mix tumbling the fish over with your hands until the seasonings are equally blended. Set the bowl in the refrigerator and allow to chill 30 minutes.

When you're ready to fry the fish, remove the fillets from the bowl one at a time and dredge in cornmeal. Use your fingers to knead the cornmeal into each fillet. Coat them well. Drop the fillets in hot peanut oil immediately as they are coated. Fry until golden brown.

CRAWFISH

Also known as crawdads or crayfish, these are mudbugs you can find in many Arkansas streams. They're also available commercially straight from Paragould through Delta Crawfish and from Hylle Crawfish Farms in Parkin.

Arkansas has several crawfish-related events, including Crawdad Days in Harrison and Crawfish Days in Dermott, both of which happen each May.

This recipe came from Chef Gary Ketchum, who was once the executive chef at the Capital Hotel, in *A Great Taste Of Arkansas: A Recipe Collection* (1986).

Fried Crawfish (Bayou Popcorn)

1 lb. crawfish tails	Flour
2 eggs	Salt and black pepper to taste
Milk	Cayenne

Season the cleaned crawfish tails with salt and pepper. Season flour with salt, pepper and cayenne. Beat the eggs and add a little milk. Dip each crawfish in the egg milk mixture and then in the flour. Fry in deep hot fat just until lightly golden. Don't overcook.

Cream gravy on biscuits at
Mel's Diner in Hot Springs.

CREAM GRAVY

A flour-and-oil gravy made just like any other gravy, with equal parts of flour and oil or butter (as grease) in the pan combined into a roux, softened by milk or cream and seasoned with salt and pepper. Cream gravy is a divine delicacy, in my honest opinion. My partner and photographer, Grav Weldon, makes it very well.

Cream Gravy or Milk Gravy

3 Tablespoons all-purpose flour
4 Tablespoons (half a stick) salted
butter, cut into eight pieces

2 ½ cups milk
¼ black pepper
Salt to taste

Toast flour in skillet over high heat, stirring constantly until it turns tan and lightly smokes. Add butter. Continue to stir constantly until all butter is melted into the paste. Remove from heat. Add pepper, reduce heat to medium, return skillet to heat. Add milk in 1/3 cup increments, continuing to stir. Remove from heat when it almost reaches desired consistency. Salt to taste.

Cream gravy and biscuits at The Sweet
and Savory Café in Eureka Springs.

CRÊPES

One of the first of a wave of magnificent new restaurants that have appeared on the Bentonville food front in the past decade, Crêpes Paulette has expanded from food truck favorite to brick-and-mortar establishment. Its handheld revolution is the inspiration of Frédéric and Paula Henry, who moved back to northwest Arkansas in 2005 from a stint in France. The Henrys opened food truck in 2010. It quickly became the go-to street food for visitors and locals alike. Both the food truck and the restaurant (which opened in 2016) offer buckwheat crêpes (naturally gluten-free) packed with a variety of fillings – from the turkey Reuben to the spicy chicken to Nutella and strawberries.

CUCUMBERS

Cultivated for more than 4000 years with roots in Central Asia, cucumbers aren't indigenous to Arkansas. But their presence here has been constant since long before statehood. The easy-to-grow, crunchy, pickle-ready vegetable has long been a favorite in gardens, in salads, relishes, pickles and such for generations.

Cucumbers grown here come in three varieties - slicing, burpless and pickling. They're grown either in elevated hills or rows, or trained along fencelines or trellises. The outer skin ranges from dark to pale green.

This recipe by Rhonda Barnes appears in *A Taste of Heaven: Fellowship Baptist Church From Our Little Kitchen Angels* (Cabot, 1999).

Tangy Tomato Cucumber Salad

2 cucumbers thinly sliced
1 teaspoon salt
2 medium tomatoes, chopped
1 medium purple onion, chopped
1/4 cup cider vinegar
2 Tablespoons oil
1 Tablespoon honey

1/2 teaspoon celery salt
1/2 teaspoon dried basil
1/2 teaspoon ground mustard
1/2 teaspoon garlic powder
1/4 teaspoon dried oregano
Dash of cayenne pepper

Place cukes in strainer, sprinkle salt and let stand for 30 minutes. Rinse well and drain. Place in a bowl. Add tomatoes and onion. In small bowl, whisk together remaining ingredients, pour over vegetables. Cover and chill for 2-3 hours. Serve with slotted spoon.

CURRY

The word curry, utilized mostly to refer to dishes made in traditional central and southeast Asian tradition, roughly means gravy - and with gravy a common comfort component around these parts, it's not far-off to note that the cuisine brings comfort to many of us in Arkansas.

Gray Weldon

No place will you find that comfort more pronounced than at Star of India. The longtime Little Rock mainstay carries an impressive menu, but two other elements truly make it shine - its extraordinary, immense yet reasonably priced seven day a week buffet, and its proprietor, the remarkable Sami Lal, who never forgets a face and greets every customer with affection and warmth. Eaters who enter after a decade's absence are still remembered by name, and gently cajoled "where have you been, my friend? It's been too long."

Popular curries at Star of India are lamb kofta, chicken tikka korma, saag paneer, pillau rices, biriyani, peshwari naan, and a lovely and extraordinary cup of chai.

CUSHAW PIE

A fine pastry crust filled with the puree of the green and white striped cushaw squash, sugar and spices. This pie is often served during the summers at Williams Tavern Restaurant at Historic Washington State Park near Hope, created from southern Arkansas family recipes. Here's that version.

Cushaw Pie

2 cups cushaw squash, pureed

2/3 cup brown sugar

1 teaspoon ground cinnamon

1/2 teaspoon ground ginger

1/2 teaspoon salt

3 large eggs

1 teaspoon vanilla

12 ounces evaporated milk

Single pie crust

Combine cushaw squash puree, brown sugar, cinnamon, ginger, and salt in a medium-size mixing bowl. Add eggs and vanilla then beat lightly with a whisk. Stir in evaporated milk. Mix well. Pour into a pastry-lined pie plate. Bake on the lowest oven rack at 375 degrees for 50-60 minutes (until a toothpick inserted in the center comes out clean). Chill before serving.

DAIRY BARS

Establishments that feature burgers and ice cream are common all across the state. Dairy bars appeared not long after Arkansas's highway system was numbered in 1926; they offer a combination of easy to pick up and go eats and treats for travelers and a hub for the commuity. Every dairy bar offers soft serve ice cream, burgers and fries; most still offer window service.

Every one of the state's 75 counties have one. Many have become legendary. For instance, the Daisy Queen in Marshall, open since 1966, is a regular stop for travelers along US Highway 65 in Searcy County. Barnett's Dairyette in Siloam Springs is known for its shakes; Susie Q's in Rogers draws in classic car enthusiasts. There's the Yellowjacket, at the main intersection in Sheridan; the Hughes Drive-In in Hughes and the Tastee Freeze in Fort Smith. You'll find the Diamond Drive-In in Clarksville still flipping burgers, while the Salem Dairy Bar just outside of Benton always has cars waiting for the window to go up and the order to be called. At Jack Allison's Polar Freeze, Jack will still tell you about the night The Beatles flew in to Walnut Ridge. And every summer, kids in swimsuits stand at the window at the Dairyette in Mt. Ida after a day on Lake Ouachita.

DANDELIONS

Some view these plants as weeds to be eradicated from a perfect lawn. Those in the know love the greens that accompany this flower as a slightly bitter accompaniment to salad - or as a component in the beloved Southern vintage, dandelion wine.

DANDY DOG

A housemade corn dog at the Atkinson's Blue Diamond Café in Morrilton, made with a Petit Jean Meats hot dog and deep fried on demand.

2 – 1 lb. packages Petit Jean hot dogs
4 ½ cups flour
3 cups corn meal
2 Tablespoons salt
2 Tablespoons baking powder
6 Tablespoons sugar
4 eggs
About 5 cups of milk or to desired consistency

Heat oil to 350 degrees. Blend all ingredients except hot dogs together. Insert wooden stick into hot dogs and dip singly into batter, completely covering each one. Fry until golden brown.

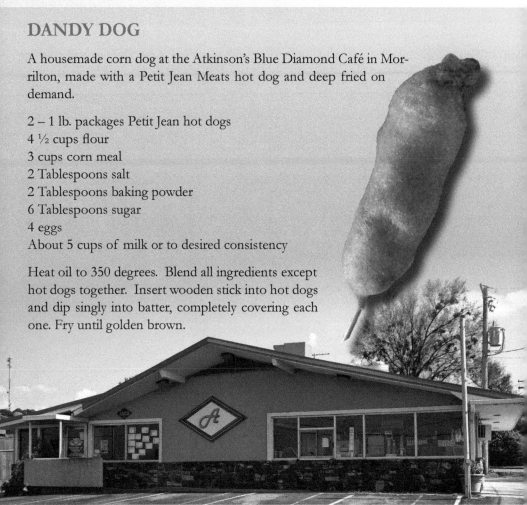

DEER

See Venison.

DEER CAMP COOKING

A tradition dating back to the 19th century, where men manning a station, cabin or tent camp would take turns creating stews and other edibles for their familial group during deer hunting trips.

DEVILED EGGS

A mainstay at any family function, these are the one-bite wonders that go first – boiled eggs, cut in half, yolks removed and blended together with other ingredients and re-stuffed into the white halves. I cannot recall my first encounter, but I do know the two truths of deviled eggs – you never make enough for a crowd, and you NEVER purchase premade deviled eggs at a store.

Basic Deviled Eggs

6 large hard-boiled eggs, peeled
2 Tablespoons mayonnaise
1 teaspoon ground mustard seed
1/2 Tablespoon sweet pickle relish

1/4 teaspoon salt
1/4 teaspoon ground black pepper
Paprika to garnish

Cut eggs in half lengthwise; remove yolks to separate bowl. Place eggs on deviled egg plate. Sprinkle a little salt on the whites.

Mix together yolks with all other ingredients except paprika. Let sit five minutes for the flavors to blend. Use a teaspoon to carefully place the yellow mixture into the whites (there will be plenty to pile on top). Sprinkle with paprika. Cover lightly with plastic wrap and refrigerate.

Deviled eggs at Stubby's BBQ in Hot Springs.

In August 2010, I was a guest at Felicia Suzanne's, a lovely upscale restaurant in downtown Memphis. Turns out, Chef Felicia Willett hails from the Upper Delta. This delightful bite drew the approval of a crowd of journalists and a spot in my culinary scrapbook. This recipe appears on the restaurant's website.

House Smoked Salmon Deviled Eggs
with Arkansas White River Caviar

1 dozen large eggs
salt
freshly ground black pepper
1/4 to 1/2 cup mayonnaise

4 ounces smoked salmon, flaked
Hot sauce
1 ounce Arkansas White River Caviar

In a saucepan, add the eggs and cover with water. Add a pinch of salt. Bring the water to a boil and cook for two minutes. Remove from heat and cover for 11 minutes. Remove eggs from water and place in a bowl of ice water. Allow eggs to sit for eight minutes.

Remove and peel the eggs. Slice each egg in half and add the yolks to a bowl. With a fork, smash all of the egg yolks. Add the mayonnaise, one spoonful at a time and mix until smooth. Season with salt and hot sauce. Fold in the smoked salmon and mix well.

**If you like your eggs creamy, add a little more mayonnaise. Place on a serving tray and garnish with caviar.

DINER FOOD

Thanks to US Highways 62, 64, 65, and 71, Arkansas developed a strong diner food culture in the 1950s and 60s. Today, diner culture still exists in Fort Smith, where three-shift operations help keep the doors open at several 24-hour breakfast joints such as Bob and Ellie's Drive-In, Lucy's Diner and Benson's Grill - the latter of which offers great diner-style decadence like The Chump and Mount Chilimonjaro (shown here).

DOUGHNUTS

There are fresh, hot doughnuts available in all but two of Arkansas's 75 counties (Chicot and Lafayette being the holdouts as of this writing). The golden rings of yeasty favor are popular around the state at doughnut shops, bakeries and a variety of grocery stores, all made on-site.

In eastern Arkansas, particularly in the Upper Delta, a variant of the filled doughnut exists where the filling is placed on top of, instead of inside, each doughnut. This variant is found at Jeri-Lyn's Donuts in Blytheville and Howard's Donuts in West Memphis.

Arkansas-based grocery chain Harp's Food Stores has its own in-house made doughnut that's achieved some fame. Martha Harps' Honey-Dipped Doughnuts have a yeastier, honey-tinged flavor than, say, Shipley's Donuts.

Most doughnut places offer varieties of cake doughnuts. And a few – such as Srown's Donuts in Bryant – delight in old fashioned, or sour cream, doughnuts. A few of Arkansas's doughnut shops offer unusual flavors – such as orange zest-filled at Community Bakery in Little Rock and chocolate fluff at Dale's Donuts in Benton. And of the state's more popular parlors, the humble Mark's Do-Nuts in North Little Rock is likely the most famous, with generously light and tangible golden morsels.

See also Spudnuts.

DRESSING

No self-respecting Arkansas cook makes "stuffing" for Thanksgiving. The perpetual annual conversation comes up between myself and photographer Grav Weldon at least once a year. His family, which hails from not only Arkansas but Oklahoma and Colorado, makes a bread-based stuffing. This is also the point in time I poke at his Okie roots.

My mom is Kitty Waldon, and her dressing is my holiday-time crack. It's come to the point where she will make extra for me to take home. And when it's gone, it's gone. Dressing was probably not meant to be a seasonal food, but for me it is a sign of the coming of the colder months only served between Thanksgiving and the New Year. Her version works in the Crock Pot.

Cornbread Dressing

1 batch cornbread (any recipe)
1 raw onion, chopped
2 sticks butter
1 cup cooked grits
1 cup chopped pecans

2 eggs
2 cans cream of chicken soup
2 Tablespoons poultry seasoning (or to taste)
Salt and pepper to taste

In a skillet, sauté onion in two sticks butter.

Crumble cornbread into Crock Pot. Pour in butter and onion from skillet. Add all other ingredients. Stir. Cook on low heat in Crock Pot for two hours, stirring occasionally. Serve as a side dish, or stir in chicken or turkey and serve as entrée.

Even better the next day.

DUCK

Stuttgart Arkansas is the Rice and Duck Capital of the World. Thousands of duck hunters flood into the Arkansas Grand Prairie every year for duck season, which traditionally runs from November through January. Wild duck is popular and has an entirely different flavor from domesticated duck.

Duck Two Ways from Brave New Restaurant, Little Rock.

Each Thanksgiving weekend, the Wings Over The Prairie Festival is held in Stuttgart. Thousands come to check out duck calls and waders and all sorts of duck hunting supplies, watch the World Championship Duck Calling Competition and its competitors from all over the world, and to experience Duck Gumbo – what can best be described as a food competition meets Mardi Gras meets the Delta (*see* Duck Gumbo).

This recipe came from *Arkansas Cooking Somehow, Somewhat, Somewhere*, put out by the American Cancer Society, Arkansas Division, Washington County Unit in 1976, part of my personal collection.

Wild Duck a la Fauvette

2 wild ducks	1/3 cup dry red wine
2 Tablespoons butter	1 teaspoon salt
2 Tablespoons sherry	¼ teaspoon black pepper
2 Tablespoons tomato paste	½ pound fresh mushrooms, sliced
2 Tablespoons flour	OR 1 8 oz. can mushrooms, drained
1 can beef bouillon (10 ounces)	1 bay leaf

Remove and discard wings from the cleaned ducks. Halve with poultry shears. Cut out the backbone completely. Melt butter in Dutch oven and brown duck halves, turning often. Pour in sherry; simmer a moment then remove ducks from pan and stir drippings well. Lower heat; add tomato paste; sift and stir in flour gradually to insure smoothness. Stir in bouillon, seasonings and wine. Bring to boil and return duck halves to pan. Add mushrooms and bay leaf. Cover and cook over very low heat for one hour. Remove duck to platter and keep warm. Strain, then degrease the sauce. Reheat sauce and spoon over duck. Serve with wild rice. Serves four.

DUCK GUMBO

The eponymous dish at the heart of the famed Duck Gombo celebration in Stuttgart is made many ways. This version by Martha Bednar of the Slovak EHC appears in *Cook's Delight: Favorite Rice Recipes Through The Years* by the Prairie County Extension Homemaker's Council (1979).

Wild Duck Gumbo

1 large or 2 small ducks (or chicken)	1 cup green onions
1 Tablespoon oil	1 cup parsley
3/4 cups bacon cut in small pieces	3 teaspoons chili powder
1 cup diced onion	1 teaspoon mustard powder
4 Tablespoons flour	1 teaspoon white pepper
4 cups hot water	1 lb. Kobasi sausage
1/2 teaspoon pepper relish	1 can shrimp
1 teaspoon seasoned salt	1 can tomatoes

Cook bacon, onions and flour to a dark brownish-red color. Add water and seasonings. Add duck (cut into chunks or frying type pieces). Boil one hour. Cut Kobasi to small pieces and add with tomatoes. Cook another hour then add shrimp. Serve over a generous bowl of hot rice.

Here's a version from Jeremy Givin in *Cooking With Pride: A Collection of Recipes by Riceland Foods* (2003).

Duck Gumbo

2 large ducks (picked is better than skinned)

2 young squirrels

1 lb. sausage of choice (Polish, summer, etc.)

4 Tablespoons flour

2 Tablespoons oil

1 stick butter

2 cups fresh or frozen okra, cut up (canned will work but do not fry)

1 can corn

1 can chicken broth

Slice of orange

1 large onion, chopped

3 cloves garlic, minced

1 or 2 cayenne peppers, chopped (optional)

2 Tablespoons Cajun seasoning

4 cups cooked long grain brown rice

3 Tablespoons scallions, chopped

1 Tablespoon Worcestershire sauce

3 quarts water

1 cup sherry

Gumbo filé

Celery salt

Salt and pepper

Put ducks and squirrels in Dutch oven with water, broth, celery salt, orange slice, onion and salt and pepper. Boil until meat is falling off the bone. Remove from btoth, skin duck and pick meat from bones, then set aside. Sauté chopped onions and garlic, then add sausage and stir until brown. Fry okra in oil about ten minutes. Make roux, using the stick of butter and flour; cook until the roux is chocolate brown. Add meat and stock (exclude orange slice, skin and bones) and all other ingredients. Bring to a boil and simmer for two to three hours. Sprinkle filé over top and enjoy. To make it Cajun hot, add a couple more peppers.

Gray Weldon

DUTCH OVEN COOKING

The Dutch oven was named the state cooking vessel in 2001. Its history goes back more than two centuries. The three-legged cast iron pot with a lid originated in the 17th century in New England. The vessel's durability and ability to absorb heat from the outside replicated the heat from traditional clay, stone and brick ovens. It's portable, relatively easy to transport and requires little maintenance.

The lidded cauldron was brought here by early settlers and was in common use by the 19th century, utilized on the hearth for cooking meals. Today, several different organizations promote Dutch oven cooking in Arkansas, and dozens of Dutch oven cook-offs are scheduled throughout the year. Instruction in cooking with the vessel are held often at several Arkansas State Parks. The ovens themselves are available through a variety of manufacturers and retail establishments, including War Eagle Mill near Rogers and the Ozark Folk Center in Mountain View.

Simple Dutch Oven Cobbler

2 cans (21 ounce) fruit pie filling of
 your choice
1 box yellow cake mix

½ cup butter or margarine
1 teaspoon cinnamon (optional)
25 charcoal briquettes

Place Dutch oven over approximately 15 hot charcoal briquettes in a fire ring or grill. Empty pie filling into Dutch oven. Shake dry cake mix over top of pie filling. Sprinkle with cinnamon (optional). Cut butter or margarine into pieces and drop on top. Put lid on and arrange 10 hot charcoal briquettes on top. Periodically lift lid with tool to check doneness (15-45 minutes, depending on heat of coals and conditions).

EDAMAME

A soybean that can be eaten as a snack, a vegetable dish or processed into sweets - the immature soybean in its pod has become extraordinarily popular, thanks to its use as a Japanese nibble and appetizer.

Edamame dates back to at least 1275 in Japan, but its adoption in western cuisine has come in just the past couple of decades, as Japanese cuisine and restaurants have moved into America. Arkansas is already one of the nation's largest soybean producers, and in 2012, Arkansas became the first state to commercially produce edamame in the U.S.

EGGPLANT

Though some have suggested the purple vegetable only caught on in Arkansas in the 20th century, recipes from the *Arkansas Gazette* indicate its presence here a century earlier. Check out the 1831 reference to fried eggplant in *Matters and Things in General*, a book published by the Arkansas Territorial Restoration Foundation (now the Historic Arkansas Museum) in 1974.

Perhaps no other eggplant dish in Arkansas is more famous than the eggplant casserole offered at Franke's Cafeteria in Little Rock. The oldest cafeteria in Arkansas, dating back to 1919, Franke's has become renown for this particular dish. I have seen many knockoffs, but this one (found in, of all things, the cookbook for the long defunct Peach's Café in Eureka Springs) is pretty spot-on.

Franke's Eggplant Casserole

1 or 2 eggplants
1 2-lb. can tomatoes or fresh to equal
1 medium onion, chopped
2 cups cornbread crumbs
½ green bell pepper, diced

2 ribs celery with leaves, washed and
  dried
2 eggs
2 ½ cups grated sharp Cheddar cheese
Cracker crumbs

Pare eggplant of blemishes (don't peel), then dice. Cook until tender in covered saucepan with a small amount of water. Drain. Wash slightly. Add salt and pepper and toss. Chop tomatoes coarsely. Mix all but one cup of the cheese together (add an egg if the mixture seems too dry). Turn into greased casserole. Top with reserve cheese and sprinkle cracker crumbs on top. Bake at 350 degrees until crumbs begin to brown.

Another version of it appears in *A Book of Favorite Recipes*, compiled by the Sheridan Jaycees (1976), submitted by Melinda Nall.

Franke's Eggplant Casserole

2 small or 1 large eggplant
½ teaspoon salt
Dash of black pepper
2 cups drained tomatoes

½ cup onion, finely chopped
2 eggs, well beaten
2 cups corn bread crumbs
Grated cheese

Peel, cube and cook eggplant in water until tender. Drain and add salt and pepper. Mash tomatoes and onions then combine with eggs and cornbread. Add to mashed eggplant. If mixture is too thick, add a little milk. Pour into buttered casserole and top with grated cheese. Bake at 375 degrees for 30 minutes.

Mrs. A. J. Godfrey submitted this recipe from the Old King Cole restaurant in Little Rock for a 1970s cookbook from Primrose United Methodist Church.

"Old King Cole" Spanish Eggplant

In 1/2 stick butter, sauté 2 cups diced onion til tender. Add one can (or fresh) tomatoes, 1 teaspoon salt, 1 teaspoon sugar and simmer til thick. Remove from fire.

Peel and cube a large eggplant. Boil until tender. Mix these two together with two slices bread toasted and crumbled and two eggs (beaten). Put in casserole with 1 cup grated cheese. Bake in moderate oven 30-40 minutes.

EGGS

A state big on chicken production should be pretty big on eggs, too, right? Indeed, there are plenty of places where eggs are produced, including several organic and commercial efforts, such as Great Day Farms and Rock Hill Foods (formerly Arkansas Egg Company). More than three billion eggs are produced for market in Arkansas each year, and more than three thousand Arkansas farm families have laying hens.

See also Deviled Eggs *and* Pickled Eggs. *Not related to* Armadillo Eggs.

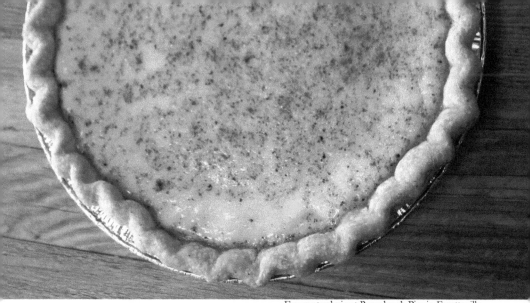

Egg custard pie at Rymolene's Pies in Fayetteville.

EGG CUSTARD PIE

A simple but rich pie with a few ingredients, usually smooth in texture with a toasted or bruleed crust. This pie actually dates back to the 15th century, from the crustade, or crusted pie, filled with a custard. In this case, the egg shines as both the means of making the custard and the overall flavor. Not to be confused with a quiche, which is a savory egg pie served at breakfast.

3 large eggs, beaten
1 cup sugar
1 teaspoon freshly grated nutmeg
1 teaspoon cornstarch

1 1/2 cups whole milk
One 9-inch deep dish pie shell, blind baked (homemade or store-bought)

Preheat oven to 350 degrees. Whisk eggs, sugar, nutmeg, cornstarch and milk together in a medium bowl until combined. Pour into pie shell and bake for 45 minutes or until pie is set; a knife inserted into the center should come out clean. Let pie cool to room temperature before serving. Refrigerate unserved portion.

Egg custard pie at BJ's Market Café in North Little Rock.

EXCALIBURGER

The Ozark Café in Jasper is the birthplace for this over-the-top burger creation, which sandwiches a half pound burger patty and an herbed mayo called Ozark Sauce between two grilled cheese sandwiches. The idea came from a couple of guys – Kyle Pounders, who would stop by the Ozark Café after rock climbing at nearby Horseshoe Canyon Ranch, and his friend Johnny, back in 2009. That ridiculously-bunned burger became an obsession, and Pounder decided to go further with it. He got the name Excaliburger trademarked, and then spent several years developing the perfect formula. Today, the Excaliburger Food Truck can sometimes be found in Little Rock - but frequently, Kyle takes his truck on the road, touring the United States. He sells a prime Creekmore beef burger between slices of toasted egg-rich challah bread (made by Old Mill Bread and Flour Co. in Little Rock) with a special sauce, lettuce, tomato and caramelized onion.

Whether or not Kyle is rambling away, the Ozark Café offers the original version of the Excaliburger for those who trek up Arkansas Scenic Highway Seven.

The Ozark Café is also home to the Deep Fried Burger and the Cheese Volcano. It's known for carrying many Arkansas specialties, including chocolate gravy and a nicely prepared Reuben.

Figs on a slice of pie at The Root Café in Little Rock.

FIGS

The fig is one of the oldest crops known to man; Arkansas is home to a variety of trees that bear the fruit, but most are kept short and tight, since temperatures below 15 degrees can damage trees. The sweet, fibrous fruit typically has two crops a year - one that grows over the winter and is harvested in spring, called the Breba crop, and one that matures in August and September. In Arkansas, the Breba crop is rare. The most popular type of fig trees here are the Celeste, which produces smaller figs with tight centers, and Brown Turkey, which has larger fruits with bigger "eyes." Figs ripen on the tree and don't last long fresh; fig preserves are a popular condiment.

FRENCH DIP

Though the French dip wasn't created in Arkansas, an incarnation of the roast beef sandwich with jus lives on at Ed Walker's Drive In, which has been serving up the sandwich to customers since 1943 on Fort Smith's Towson Avenue. It's a tender mess of fall-apart slow-simmered roast beef on a tight French roll served with a savory housemade jus for dipping..

Ed Walker's Drive In is, incidentally, the only place in Arkansas where you can get beer delivered to you, curbside. It's also home to the largest cheeseburger in Arkansas.

FRIED BOLOGNA

Zagat, of all organizations, named the fried bologna sandwich as Arkansas's entry into its *50 States, 50 Sandwiches* story. While yes, many of us grew up on fried bologna, it's a stretch. Best example of the sandwich may be the version served with an inch of bologna at Feltner's Whatta-Burger in Russellville, though it's also a popular dish at the Southfork Restaurant in Gurdon. Barbecue versions can be found at Sim's Barbecue in Little Rock and Kibb's BBQ in Pine Bluff.

When I was a young child, bologna for frying was always obtained at Breitweiser's Meat Market in Benton. Breitweiser's still smokes a great deal of meat, and the bologna is always fantastic.

How to properly fry bologna

Place a skillet over high heat.

Slice your bologna ¼ to 1 inch thick (or have your butcher do it in advance). Cut out from the center to the edge on one side. Place in hot skillet.

When the meat develops bubbling and the edge begins to char, flip bologna and cook the other side. Remove from pan and repeat with any additional bologna.

Purists will tell you to put the bologna directly on white bread to absorb the grease. If you prefer your bologna with a condiment, spread the mayo, mustard or Miracle Whip directly on both slices before applying bologna. It makes a seal to keep your sandwich bread from getting soggy.

See also Barbecue Bologna.

FRIED CABBAGE

Sliced or cut into chunks, sautéed with butter or bacon grease in a skillet until translucent and served hot. fried cabbage is a frequent side dish found all over the state. The heating process brings out the natural sweetness, much like caramelizing onions. Some add a little hot sauce for flavor.

This recipe by Lou Brummitt appears in *The Better To Serve III: Golden Anniversary Edition* (1997) by the Amici Club of Stuttgart.

Fried Cabbage

1 head cabbage
1 bell pepper
1 small onion
6 slices bacon

Cut vegetables into chunks. Soak in ice water one hour. Fry bacon until crisp. Remove and drain on paper towel. While grease is still hot, shake vegetables from water and drop into hot skillet carefully (will splatter on you). Cover; lower heat and stir occasionally until crisp. To serve, crumble bacon over top.

Fried cabbage at R.A. Pickens
and Son Commissary
in Pickens, south of Dumas.

FRIED CHICKEN AND SPAGHETTI

A singular pairing of dishes has become the signature meal of the Arkansas Ozarks. But its origins go back to Italy and to Lake Village. In 1895 and 1897, a group of Italian immigrants bought into the idea of Sunnyside Plantation. New York philanthropist Austin Corbin had contacted the mayor of Rome to find buyers. Corbin planned to sell ten- and twelve-acre plots to new area colonists with payments stretched out over several years. Those who bought in came by ship to Ellis Island, became citizens, got back on a boat and were brought up the Mississippi to their new home near present-day Lake Village. These new arrivals became tenant farmers, and though they had planned to come to America and grow fresh produce, they discovered that slow transportation in the area and the type of soil they had to deal with was far more suitable to cotton and corn—neither of which these farmers knew much about. Add in the humid climate, mosquitoes and disease, and you have a recipe for failure. One hundred and twenty five members died in the first year.

Over the couple of years they were in Chicot County, these immigrants shared their Italian gastronomic identity, teaching pasta and sauce making to the residents, and picked up the knowledge of how to properly prepare poultry for the pan, soul food style.

The hard life was too much for many of the new immigrants.. In 1898, Father Pietro Bandini set out to find better conditions. He traveled by horseback along the Arkansas River and into the Ozarks. He eventually found a place much more like the land at his original home, and he sent word back. Forty families followed and settled in the new community, Tontitown, which was named after 17th century explorer Henri de Tonti. The families came in waves starting in January, not the best time of year to start a farm. By March, the community had its first death but also its first birth, and its members were hopeful.

They grew apples, peaches, strawberries, whatever vegetables they could force up through the rocky soil and eventually turned to the grapes that would make the town famous—yes, grapes.

It wasn't easy. Ozark natives didn't take well to the Italian immigrants at first, but the tenacity of these tightknit families was undeniable and, quite frankly, admirable. And that fried chicken and spaghetti combination, irresistible and served up with bread and butter, over time brought the masses to the restaurants that were born from the Tontitown settlement.

Today, Tontitown's oldest restaurant is The Venesian Inn. Originally opened on June 28th, 1947, the original wooden tables installed by Germano Gasparotto are still within. The fried chicken and spaghetti combination is the restaurant's most popular offering, with extraordinarily juicy chicken and mounds of spaghetti folded into a spicy sauce, served with soaked salad, fat trefoil or clover shaped dinner rolls and butter. Other longtime purveyors include the AQ Chicken House in Springdale (AQ stands for Arkansas Quality) and Mama Z's in Tontitown.

The combination is also the star of the show at the famed Italian dinners served each August at the Tontitown Grape Festival. The long-running festival commemorates the original Italian settlers to the area with a week's worth of entertainment, vendors, concerts, and a midway where the entire community comes to have a good time.

FRIED GREEN TOMATOES

Popularized in Frannie Flagg's famed book *Fried Green Tomatoes at the Whistlestop Café*, fried green tomatoes have been an occasional side dish on Arkansas summer tables for generations. Slices of fresh green tomatoes battered with cornmeal are skillet fried for a tart snack. Some folks use egg or milk, some folks use flour, and some use a combination. Cotham's in Scott was known for using just seasoned cornmeal for its mix; this version is still available at Cotham's in the City in Little Rock.

Cotham's Mercantile's Fried Green Tomatoes

Green tomatoes (no red tomatoes)
Cotham's Catfish Seasoning or seasoned cornmeal
Oil

Slice tomatoes 1/8th inch thick. Soak slices in ice water for about 5 minutes. Heat at least an inch of oil in skillet or deep fryer to 350 degrees. Take tomatoes out of water, coat with catfish seasoning or cornmeal, and fry for around 8 minutes, turning once. Drain, then serve with ranch dressing.

FRIED PICKLES

The creation of Bernell Austin at the long-gone Duchess Drive-In, fried pickles have spread throughout the United States as a fair food, greasy spoon standard and pub standard. But the original certainly came out of Atkins.

Atkins was once known as the Pickle Capital of the World. In 1945, the Goldsmith Pickle Company located a plant in the town. Fifteen years later, Bernell Austin leased a parcel of land from the Griffin Oil Company for 10 dollars a month, right across from the plant. He built the Duchess Drive-In there, a pink and purple edifice where plant employees could come get lunch..

Austin, known as "Fats" or "Fatman" to many of his constituents, looked for ways to increase business. In 1963, he struck on a new idea, battering and deep-frying hamburger dill slices and selling them for 15 cents for a basket of 15. The fried pickle was born.

Austin wasn't happy with that first recipe. He tweaked it and eventually settled on slicing dill pickles into planks and dropping them into a spicy batter before deep frying them to a golden brown. The recipe remains a family secret, though many claim that the Old South in Russellville has the formula. Some 2500 orders of fried pickles are served each May at the Atkins Pickle Festival.

Fried Pickles
Stephanie Wilson

1 egg	½ cup cornmeal
1 teaspoon dill weed, divided	½ cup all-purpose flour
6 to 8 kosher dill spears, brine reserved	Salt and pepper

Beat your egg, adding a ½ teaspoon of the dill weed and about a tablespoon of the pickle brine. Mix the cornmeal and flour, adding the other ½ teaspoon of dill weed and salt and pepper to taste.

Dredge the pickles in the cornmeal and flour. Coat them in the egg mixture and then dredge in the cornmeal and flour again. Freeze for about an hour. Deep fry these until golden brown and serve with ranch dressing.

Fried Pickles
Kat Robinson

1 cup all-purpose flour	½ cup water
¼ cup rice flour or cornstarch	½ cup pickle juice
1 teaspoon baking powder	1 egg yolk
¼ teaspoon salt	4 cups dill pickles in ¼-inch slices
¼ teaspoon pepper	Oil for frying

Sift dry ingredients together in a bowl. In a separate bowl, whisk liquids and egg yolk together and then incorporate into dry ingredients. Set in the refrigerator for 30 minutes to one hour.

Heat oil to 375 degrees. Working with about a ¼ of the pickles at a time, drop slices into batter and stir around. Using a slotted spoon, remove from batter and carefully place into hot oil. Fry one to two minutes (like fried okra). Serve warm.

FRIED PIES

The folded over pie is nothing new in this world. Like many food traditions, the idea of taking something and putting it in dough dates back to antiquity. Putting something inside something else made of flour goes back to Roman times. In the Middle Ages, food was often baked in flour coffins… no, not like you put bodies in. A coffin was a baking container made of a flour dough. These coffins weren't very tasty. They were usually thick so the food inside them would cook without burning, and when the meal was over they'd be given to the poor as scraps. In the northeast and around the Great Lakes, there have been pies known as pasties (pronounced PAH-stees), for generations. These were big hand pies full of something savory, like stew. There's even a variation in New England where cooks would tuck a bit of jam or some sweetened fruit into the end of the big pies. They were easy to transport and made the perfect working man food.

Fried pies can be found all over Arkansas, from fine dining establishments to truck stops. The crust can be thin or thick, crusty or crisp. Variations are made with traditional pie crust, biscuit dough, bread dough and even doughnut dough.

Ozark Folk Center Fried Pies

3 ounces evaporated milk	2 cups self-rising flour
1/2 cup water	1/2 cup plain flour
1/2 cup shortening, melted	2 cans (21 ounces each) pie filling or
1 oz. white vinegar	42 ounces homemade pie filling

Mix together evaporated milk, water, shortening, and white vinegar. Blend in flour. Using an electric mixer, mix until texture of dough is silky, not sticky or dry. Adjust with small amounts of liquid if too dry to roll or flour if sticky.

Pull an amount the size of a big walnut and roll into ball. Roll this to a 6" circle on floured board or parchment paper. Place four ounces of any type of filling towards one side of the circle. Brush the edges of the circle with evaporated milk. Fold in half and seal edges with fork or fingers. Punch two holes in the top using a fork. This prevents explosion.

Use vegetable oil to deep fry at temperature of 350 degrees for five minutes or until golden brown. If pan frying, turn pies when first side browns.

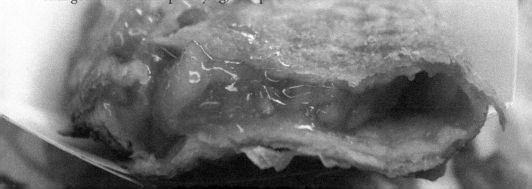

FRIED RICE

Considering our preponderance of rice and the fact that Arkansas produces more than half the rice grown in the United States, it should come as no surprise that fried rice is common here. It appears in cookbooks all through the 20th century in all manners of flavors and ranges, from bacon and green bean versions to Asian representations, the latter likely influenced by a Chinese population that came to the Arkansas Delta at the end of the 19th century.

Ten ingredient fried rice at
Go Go China in Little Rock.

FRITO CHILI PIE

It's up for debate, but Claude Spradlin Jr. makes a good case that the Frito chili pie may have first been created at Spradlin's Dairy Delight in England. Long disputed between Texas and New Mexico, Spradlin's owner says his dad came up with the eponymous dish. Back in 1957, Claude Spradlin started up Spradlin's Dairy Delight. His son, Claude Spradlin, Jr., took over in 1973.

Spradlin, Jr. says his dad actually came up with the Frito chili pie back when the restaurant started -- and that the folks at the Frito Lay Corporation actually sent him a letter thanking him for his contribution and the creation of the dish. It was sold in a paper boat for 15 cents -- a nickel for the Fritos and a dime for the chili -- and it was very popular.

Several sources claim that the dish was first served in the 1960s by Theresa Hernandez at the Woolworth Five and Dime Store's lunch counter in Santa Fe, New Mexico. Others claim the mother of Frito founder Charles Elmer Doolin came up with the original -- and that Daisy Dean Doolin fashioned many Fritos dishes all the way back in the 1930s. The recipe itself was printed on Fritos bags back in 1962 and credited to Nell Morris.

BBQ Smoked Frito Pie at Mean Pig BBQ in Cabot.

Regardless of where it was created or by whom, the Frito chili pie is part of Arkansas dairy bar cuisine. Want to make a big one at home for the family? Here's the official recipe from Frito Lay.

Frito Chili Pie

1 large bag of FRITOS® Original Corn Chips
1 15-ounce can of chili with beef (with or without beans), heated
1 8-ounce bag of shredded cheese
Optional: chopped onion, tomatoes, lettuce, jalapeños and/or sour cream

In an oven-safe serving dish, pour in FRITOS® Original Corn Chips and spread evenly. Heat chili and pour evenly over corn chips. Add additional ingredients like onion, tomato, lettuce, and jalapeño as desired. Sprinkle cheese all over and pop into the oven at 350 degrees till the cheese is a little melted. Serve immediately.

FRUITCAKES

Habib's, opened by a Lebanese immigrant in downtown Helena in 1888, became quite famous for its fruitcakes. The dense-packed confection was packed in a tin and shared all over the country. The tins showed how bourbon could be utilized to help, ahem, preserve the cake's moistness.

FRUIT PUNCH

I'm not for an instant suggesting that fruit punch is an Arkansas creation. But we do have a particular sort of fruit punch that's almost always sold with Ark-Mex foods. This punch is well known for being served at Mexico Chiquito, the restaurant franchise best known for its longstanding association with the first cheese dip. It's also served each year at the Arkansas State Fair, and there are few better thirst quenchers around.

Arkansas State Fair Style Fruit Punch

1 (46 ounce) can pineapple juice
1 (1 liter) bottle grenadine syrup
1 cup white sugar
1/4 cup lemon juice
1 (1 ounce) packet instant tea powder
5 quarts water

Mix pineapple juice, grenadine, sugar, lemon juice, and instant tea powder together in a two-gallon container; stir to dissolve sugar and tea powder. Add water, stir. If flavor is too strong, add water.

Each October, thousands come out to the Arkansas State Fairgrounds for the largest gathering in the state – the Arkansas State Fair and Livestock Show. While many come just for the rides, the food and the concerts, the fair itself was built on friendly competition and an effort to showcase the best of Arkansas.

In fact, the fair began not as a way to entertain the public, but to showcase an important part of the agricultural world. After the University of Arkansas Cooperative Extension Service found through a survey that livestock would likely be successful as an Arkansas agricultural venture, a group of individuals created an exposition to showcase what was here. The first Arkansas Livestock Show was held in November 1938 in North Little Rock. Though it lost money, the idea had been planted. The next year the event was moved to mid-October for better weather, and famed cowboy crooner Roy Rogers was brought in for entertainment. Thus the Arkansas State Fair was established. It was moved to its permanent site along Roosevelt Road in 1945 and remains there to this day.

Since then, such attractions as the latest amusement rides, concerts featuring popular musical acts (from Gene Autry and Johnny Cash to Bret Michaels and Rick Springfield) and outrageous food have spread throughout the fairgrounds over the 11 day course of events. But at the heart of the fair lies the same commitment to supporting agricultural interests, livestock and friendly competition as in its early days.

FUDGE

The famed sweet confection was a popular offering at many of the roadside tourist shops along highways in the Ozarks for decades. The candy made from sugar, butter, milk and additional ingredients could be made in large batches and transported well without refrigeration. Over the course of generations, many of those roadside stops (which also often sold smoked meats, jams and jellies, local produce and crafts) closed down, but a handful still offer the sweets, including Sweet's Fudge and Two Dumb Dames in Eureka Springs, PattiCakes Bakery in Conway and Pickles Gap Village near Conway.

This recipe comes from Pete Pleva in the book *Arkansas Recipes, Legends & Such: Pickles Gap, Skunk Hollow and Toad Suck,* compiled by Janis Carolyn Mack.

Fabulous Fudge

2 ¼ cups sugar
¾ cups evaporated milk
16 large marshmallows
   or 1 cup marshmallow crème
¼ cup butter or margarine

¼ teaspoon salt
6 ounces semi-sweet chocolate chips
   (1 cup)
1 teaspoon vanilla
1 cup nuts, chopped (optional)

Mix sugar, evaporated milk, marshmallows, butter and salt in a heavy medium saucepan. Cook, stirring constantly, over medium heat, bringing it to an all over boil. Boil and stir five minutes. Stir in chocolate until completely melted. Add vanilla and nuts. Spread in buttered 8-inch square pan. Cool. Cut into 30 pieces.

GAR

The gar is a type of needlefish that populates many Arkansas waterways. They are not, in general, considered good eating by the majority of folks who fish our lakes and streams. Four species - the longnose, the shortnose, the spotted and the alligator gar - can be found in shallower areas. While the fish produce great sport for anglers, few bother to spend the effort to hack through the tough scales. Gar eggs are also poisonous to man. However, some do extract the backstrap for use in small steaks or grind them to be used in patties.

THE GARDEN (sandwich)

Jimmy's Serious Sandwiches doesn't advertise much. It doesn't need to. The Midtown eatery is usually packed with folks from every walk of life during the lunch hour. Many of them come for The Garden, a carefully constructed vegetarian sandwich that comes across as a filling, satisfying sandwich without an ounce of meat. Back in 1979, Jimmy Wiseman's creation won the first place in the National Sandwich Contest. Though the recipe for the sandwich is actually posted on the wall next to the door, few actually make it at home. They'd rather get their fix in the restaurant or in a lunch box to go.

The Garden

2 (10 ounce) packages frozen chopped spinach, thawed
½ cup minced green onion
6 Tablespoons mayonnaise
1 Tablespoon minced bell pepper
1 Tablespoon lemon juice
¼ teaspoon salt
12 slices pumpernickel bread
¼ cup butter or margarine, softened

½ lb. fresh mushrooms, sliced OR one 2.5 ounce can mushrooms
1 Tablespoon butter or margarine
¾ cup fresh alfalfa sprouts, washed and drained
2 Tablespoons sunflower seeds
6 slices provolone cheese
6 slices cheddar cheese
6 slices Swiss cheese

Squeeze spinach to remove excess liquid; combine spinach and the next six ingredients (green onion through salt) in a bowl; stir to combine; set aside. Sauté mushrooms in one tablespoon butter in a skillet until tender; set aside. Spread one teaspoon softened butter on one side of each bread slice. Lightly brown six bread slices, buttered side down, on a hot griddle; remove from heat. Spread spinach mixture evenly on unbuttered sides of toasted bread; sprinkle with alfalfa sprouts, mushrooms, and sunflower kernels; set aside.

Place one slice each of provolone, cheddar, and Swiss cheese on unbuttered side of remaining bread slices. Place bread, buttered side down, on hot griddle; cook over medium heat, just until cheese softens and bread lightly browns.

To serve, put cheese-topped bread slices and spinach-topped slices together to make sandwiches.

GARLIC

Dozens of varieties of this glorious bulb grow in Arkansas, not just in gardens but in the wild, where it likely sprouts on the sites of former homesteads. Hardy, easy to raise, the cloves are one of the most common flavoring agents in all of cooking, not just in Arkansas.

Little Rock entrepreneur Amy Bradley-Hole shares her love of Tuscan cooking with a garlic sauce she manufactures and sells. Bonta Toscana garlic sauce was originally a quiet secret shared with some of Arkansas's most devout food lovers by Bradley-Hole - now it's available through a variety of local retailers. The garlic-tomato sauce is light and high on flavor.

Fried chicken gizzards at Walker's Dairy Bar in Marked Tree.

GIZZARDS

While folks in other states use this chicken portion for fish bait, here in Arkansas we batter and fry it and serve it up hot. You'll find gizzards on the menu at family restaurants like the esteemed AQ Chicken House in Springdale, at dairy bars like Walker's Dairy Bar in Marked Tree, and in gas stations with hot food stands all over the state.

Chicken Gizzards

1 pound chicken gizzards, rinsed
2 stalks celery, chopped
1 onion, chopped
1 bay leaf
1 1/2 teaspoons celery salt, divided
1 teaspoon seasoning salt
1/2 teaspoon ground black pepper

1/2 teaspoon dried Italian seasoning
1 teaspoon garlic powder
1/4 teaspoon ground cumin
1/2 teaspoon Louisiana-style hot sauce
3 cups oil for deep frying
1 cup all-purpose flour

Place chicken gizzards, celery, onion, bay leaf, and 1 teaspoon of celery salt into a saucepan. Pour in enough water to cover the gizzards. Bring to a boil, reduce heat to low, cover, and simmer until tender, about 2 1/2 hours. Add more water during simmering, if needed, to keep gizzards covered. Remove gizzards to a bowl. Discard the celery, onion and bay leaf. Reserve broth.

Season gizzards with remaining dry spices and hot sauce, stirring to combine. Pour 1/3 cup of the reserved broth over the seasoned gizzards, and refrigerate for 30 minutes or more, stirring often. Drain.

Heat oil in a deep-fryer or large saucepan to 375 degrees F (190 degrees C). Place flour in a plastic bag. Add gizzards. Shake the bag to thoroughly coat gizzards with flour. Gently lower about 1/4 of the gizzards into the hot oil, and fry until golden brown, about five minutes per batch. Drain on paper towels. Serve hot.

GRAPES

Grapes come in endless varieties, colors and sweetness. They can be used for wines, in jams and jellies and even breads and cakes. Their juice is sweet, and they're the main component in wine. Grapes are grown sporadically throughout the state, with vineyards prominent in Arkansas's viticultural region around Altus and juice grapes grown in the area near Tontitown.

You may not know this, but Arkansas has an official state grape. It's the Cynthiana, the oldest North American grape in cultivation today. First identified in 1770, it's often referred to as the "Cabernet of the Ozarks." Similar to the Norton grape, the Cynthiana is winter-hardy and highly disease-resistant. It's used in deep red wines and is credited with being a great artery de-clogger. Several of our state's wineries utilize Cynthiana grapes in their wines, particularly Post Familie, Mount Bethel, Château Aux Arc and Keel's Creek.

Arkansas is also the oldest grape juice and wine producing state in the southern United States. Two wineries, Wiederkehr Wine Cellar and Post Familie Vineyards, started off in 1880 in the Altus region of the state. Today, these wineries along with Mount Bethel and Châteaux Aux Arc offer tours and tastings.

While our state's wineries grow a good portion of the grapes in this state for wine use, there are also several edible varieties available to just pick up and eat. Dahlem Vineyard in Altus offers several varieties of table grapes, including Mars and Venus. The Mars varietal is a sturdy and stout grape, while the more delicate and much sweeter Venus variety has more flavor in its peel.

See also Muscadines *and* Wine.

Altus also offers the Altus Grape Festival the last Friday and Saturday of each July. There, you can sample grapes, juice and wine, participate in a grape stomp or the grape pie eating contest, dress like Bacchus for a prize and listen to local country, folk and bluegrass music at the gazebo. This recipe is for a double crust grape pie.

Altus Grape Pie

Crust:
2 1/2 cups flour
1/4 cups sugar
1/4 lb. plus 2 teaspoons butter
2 egg yolks
1/4 cup water

Filling
2 lbs. black or red table grapes
1/4 cups sugar
2 Tablespoons flour
1 Tablespoon sugar (optional)

Stir together all dry ingredients Add butter and cut it into flour until it resembles coarse meal. Stir in yolks, and if needed a tiny amount of water. Mix dough just enough to combine the ingredients. Chill one hour. Roll out 2/3 of dough and line a standard pie pan. Chill remaining dough and pie pan.

Remove seeds from grapes and air dry in a colander for one hour. Mix flour and sugar. Toss grapes in flour-sugar mixture, then pour into unbaked pie shell.

Heat oven to 350 degrees. Roll out remainder of dough and place atop pie. Cut slits into pie crust to allow steam to escape. Bake for 60-70 minute or until a little juice bubbles through the slits in the crust. Remove from oven. Sprinkle large granule sugar over the top. Allow to cool one hour before serving.

GRAPETTE

One of the original Fook's Flavors, this grape-flavored soft drink was first produced and marketed in 1939 in Camden by Benjamin Tyndle Fooks. The soft drink started off as a syrup added to a carbonated base. It was eventually bottled like more traditional beverages. In 1962, Grapette International was formed, and produced the dark purple beverage (along with Orangette, Lemonette and other flavors). Through a series of acquisitions, Grapette and its sister flavors ended up with Monarch Company, which produced NuGrape, in 1977. The product disappeared from domestic shelves (though it did continue overseas) after that, and was not produced here for a decade.

Turns out, Grapette was Sam Walton's favorite beverage. In the late 1980s, Walton met with Grapette International chairman Brooks Rice and straight out asked for Grapette for his stores. Though the product could not be sold under the Grapette name, the formulas and flavors become the basis for Sam's Choice sodas sold through Walmart and other Walton properties. Grapette and Orangette have been sold since 2005 under their original names through Walmart. Both are manufactured in Malvern these days. You can still find Grapette on tap in Camden at Wood's Place.

GRAVY

The *Merriam-Webster Dictionary* defines gravy as "a sauce made from the thickened and seasoned juices of cooked meat," "something additional or unexpected that is pleasing or valuable." For Arkansas eaters, gravy is more than a condiment, just shy of a main course in itself, a pile of potatoes or rice or biscuits away from all one needs to consume in a quick and delicious meal.

There are so many types of gravy served in Arkansas, from brown gravy to cream gravy, red gravy, red-eye gravy, sausage gravy, chicken gravy, even chocolate gravy. The only true common elements between the types are flour or flour substitute, a fat like butter or grease, and a skillet. We tend to put far less emphasis on roux color than our neighbors in Louisiana. *See* Brown Gravy, Chocolate Gravy, Cream Gravy, Red Gravy, *and* Red-Eye Gravy.

GREEK FOOD FESTIVAL

The International Greek Food Festival is held each year on the second weekend in May at the Annunciation Greek Orthodox Church in West Little Rock. It's the largest ethnic food festival in the state, a celebration of the delicious, unique, and exciting food and culture of the Mediterranean, benefiting local charities. Members of the church begin making baklava for the event right after Christmas, baking tens of thousands of pieces of baklava alongside kourambiethes, sourota, loukomathes and other pastries over the course of several months. They're always gone before the festival closes. Hungry attendees can enjoy gyros, leg of lamb, pastitsio and other savory delights while watching dancing or perusing the Greek market. There's even a drive-thru, and a local delivery service will bring a taste of Greek to most Little Rock addresses.

GREEN BEANS

Often referred to as bush beans or bunch beans, these legumes originated in Mexico and have been cultivated in Arkansas more than 200 years. They're also called snap beans, since more recent cultivars lack the fibrous threads that were once referred to as string beans (though string beans are also still cultivated in rural gardens). Many an Arkansas youngster has spent time pulling the green pods off the bushy plants. The long pods are typically snapped into segments of one or two inches and boiled up with a chunk of bacon or salt pork fat. Other preparations include steaming or stewing.

Here's a recipe from *Secrets of the South* (1993) by Alice May Johnson of Gillett.

Fresh Green Beans

2 pounds fresh green beans
4 slices bacon, diced
1 medium onion, chopped
2 cups water

1 teaspoon salt
1/2 teaspoon sugar
1/2 teaspoon black pepper

Wash and snap beans into 1 to 1 1/2 inch sized pieces. Fry bacon in a large Dutch oven. Add onions and fry until browning begins. Add green beans and remaining ingredients. Heat to boiling, then cover pan. Lower heat and simmer for 90 minutes or until beans are tender. Yields six to eight servings.

GREEN TOMATO RELISH (Green Tomato Pickles)

Green tomato relish/green tomato pickle. Part condiment, part pickle, this canned fruit becomes the perfect accompaniment to fried catfish. You can purchase the condiment or make your own. My aunt Wava Gail would use this recipe:

Wava's Green Tomato Pickles

Half a peck of green tomatoes, quartered

12 medium onions, chopped

1 cup salt

3 bell peppers, chopped

4 cups sugar

1 (16 ounce) bottle white vinegar

1 Tablespoon peppercorns

4 Tablespoons mustard seed

4 Tablespoons celery seed

2 Tablespoons whole cloves

3 cinnamon sticks

Combine tomatoes, onions and salt in large container; let stand overnight. Rinse tomatoes and onions in cold water; drain. Place in large stockpot. Add peppers, sugar and vinegar. Place remaining ingredients in spice bag or tied cheesecloth and drop into liquid. Stir over medium heat until sugar dissolves. Boil rapidly for 12 minutes. Remove spice bag. Pack in hot jars. Makes four quarts or eight pints.

Catfish Hole Green Tomato Pickles

2 quarts quartered green tomatoes

2 cups chopped onion

1/3 cup chopped hot peppers

1/3 cup chopped red bell peppers

1/3 cup celery, chopped

2 cups sugar

3 Tablespoons salt

3 cups apple cider vinegar

1 teaspoon celery seed

1/4 teaspoon yellow mustard seed

Combine ingredients in a large pot and bring to a slow boil. Let simmer for about 5 minutes. Ladle into hot, sterile jars, wipe lip edge of jars, screw on hot, new jar rings and flats and lightly tighten. Place into a boiling water bath, with at least 1/2 inch of water above the jar lids. Bring to a boil; keep slowly boiling for 15 minutes. Remove and let cool overnight, then label and store for at least two weeks.

Green tomato pickles at Catfish Hole in Alma.

HAM

There was a time when great smokehouses dotted the land, especially in Arkansas's Ozark and Ouachita regions. A few of the old-time ham smokers still remain, such as Burl's Country Smokehouse in Royal and Coursey's Smoked Meats in St. Joe. Ham's the meat for barbecue at Walnut Ridge's popular Polar Freeze. Of course, the big ham in the market is Petit Jean Meats, though you can also order a fine variety through Burge's.

Above: A ham on the cutting board at Coursey's Smoked Meats in St. Joe.

Right: A recipe from Wison's Meat Cookery (1921).

Left: Hams curing on a rack at Petit Jean Meats in Morrilton.

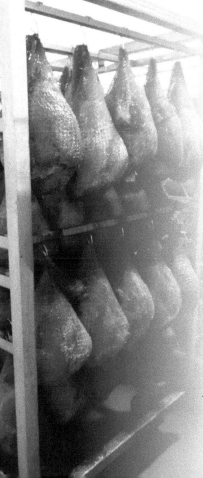

ARKANSAS HAM—Cook thin slices of ham in hot frying pan until slightly browned. Remove to hot platter. To the fat in the pan add the following mixture well beaten:

3 tablespoons vinegar
1½ teaspoons mustard
1½ teaspoons sugar
Paprika

When mixture is thoroughly heated, pour over ham and serve at once. Ham cut about one-half inch thick is sometimes preferred to the thin slices.

How to heat a Petit Jean Meats ham in the dishwasher

Note: Petit Jean Meats packs its hams in a special three-layer sealed plastic casing, which allows for heating without water contact with the ham.

Place your Petit Jean Half Spiral Sliced Ham (in the bag) face down on the bottom rack of your dishwasher. Be sure not to puncture the packaging as it is essential to holding in the juices. Set your dishwasher to the "Heavy Wash" or "Pots and Pans" setting. Press Start. Once the wash cycle is done, you should have a little wear on the label and a very clean ham package. Remove packaging and your ham is ready to slice and eat.

*Standard residential water heaters come pre-set at 120 degrees F. Petit Jean Meats does not recommend heating your ham in a dishwasher if you have modified your factory settings on your water heater, or cooking other items in the dishwasher.

HICKORY NUTS

The drupaceous nut of the hickory tree, these woody-hulled "hicker-nuts" are filled with a nutmeat similar to pecan. They're harder to crack than pecans, and they're often harvested by squirrels before humans can get at them. You'll need a hammer to crack them.

HONEY

Yes, honey is available anywhere. But we utilize it well here in Arkansas. Many of our older restaurants offer a bottle of honey on their tables alongside sugar, pepper sauce, salt and pepper. It's used on biscuits, in doughnut glazing, in barbecue sauce and salad dressings. It's drizzled into sopapillas, onto peanut butter sandwiches and even eaten in candy sticks.

For decades, a lone honesty honey stand has stood in front of a house south of Damascus on US Highway 65. The stand (and once, the honey that was sold there) was Garland Gilliland's. Originally from Alabama, Gilliland once sold beekeeping equipment from a Conway hardware store before starting The Honey House in

Damascus with his wife. He helped start the Ozark Foothills Beekeeping Association and mentored dozens of young beekeepers. When the store started getting in the way of his beekeeping, the gentleman beekeeper and his wife started that honesty honey stand with honey, sorghum, bee pollen, jams and jellies. Mr. Gilliland passed away in 2009, but the family keeps the stand open to this day.

The oldest and largest honey distributor in Arkansas is Fischer's Honey. Its history goes back to a family kitchen where beekeeper Raymond Fischer would put honey he harvested in jars and take out to give away or sell in the 1920s. His little operation soon outgrew the kitchen, so he moved it first to the garage, and then the basement. In the 1930s a little honey plant was built. Today a 20,000 square foot facility in a North Little Rock neighborhood processes honey from beekeepers and producers from a large area to satisfy demand.

In the 2010s, backyard beekeeping has become a popular endeavor around Arkansas, with classes and mentoring programs being shared. Many of those small operations are producing honey for sale through Arkansas Grown and other agricultural endeavors.

HOTEL GOLDMAN

From its opening in 1910 to the early 1960s, this edifice was the finest lodging and dining Fort Smith had to offer.

The Fort Smith Museum of History preserves much of the hotel's heritage in an exhibit on its second floor. We also have records of what was served at its white glove, silver tray restaurant, thanks to preserved menus. Some may be surprised to find that during the 1930s it sold egg and olive, cheese and jelly and other simple sandwiches right alongside Kansas City steaks and oyster and shrimp cocktails.

HUBCAP BURGERS

Arkansas burger makers have long since adopted a particular style of hamburger, where large patties of a pound (or more!) are placed between buns the size of an automobile hubcap.

The most famous of these was the Hub Cap Burger from Cotham's Mercantile, built in 1912 at Scott. Though the store had been around for ages, it wasn't until it was "discovered" by Senator David Pryor and (then) Governor Bill Clinton in the 1980s that business really took off. Sadly, the original Cotham's was lost to fire in May 2017. However, its sister property, Cotham's in the City, continues to offer much of the original menu at its location on Third Street, not far from the Arkansas State Capitol in Little Rock.

HUSH PUPPIES

The default side for catfish, often created from leftover catfish batter and egg, hush puppies received their name from cooks who would throw those bits of fried batter to the dogs to keep them quiet while everyone else enjoyed their catfish. The best I've found have been at Catfish Hole in Alma, though the ones served at the annual Grady Fish Fry are also very good.

From Dondie's White River Princess in Des Arc, this recipe was originally featured on the Arkansas Tourism website.

Dondie's Hush Puppies

2 cups self-rising cornmeal
2 cups self-rising flour
1/2 teaspoon salt
3 Tablespoons sugar
3 large eggs, slightly beaten

1/2 cup milk
1 large onion, chopped
2 jalapeño peppers, seeded and chopped

Combine first four ingredients in large bowl, combine eggs and milk - add to dry ingredients, stir until moistened then add onions and peppers and mix. Drop by tablespoon into hot oil; cook for three minutes or until golden brown.

Here's a cheesy variant found in *Minuteman's Mate's Mess*, contributed by Mary Jo Horton, compiled in 1977 by the officer's wives of the Arkansas National Guard.

Central High Cafeteria Hush Puppies

Hush puppies at Catfish Hole in Alma.

2 cups cornmeal
1 cup flour
6 Tablespoons baking powder
½ teaspoon salt
1 teaspoon sugar
1 cup grated cheese
3 eggs
1 grated onion
Buttermilk

Combine all ingredients except buttermilk. Add buttermilk until the batter reaches the right consistency. Drop into hot vegetable oil by spoonfuls; cook until golden brown.

When speaking of hush puppies, it's important for one to be aware of a grand gathering each August in the little burg of Grady, just off US Highway 65. There, at E.C. "Ned" Hardin's farmstead on the third Thursday in August, hundreds consume catfish, fries, slaw and melon together while reconnecting with Grady-ites and politicians and listening to the sound of the Cummins Prison Band. This is the Grady Fish Fry - a 60 plus year tradition that funds scholarships for area students, and draws attendees from all over the state.

A longstanding wood beamed pavilion stands over dozens of men who in turn hover over deep fryers with slotted metal spatulas and spider baskets, pulling round after round of cornmeal-coated catfish out onto trays. Those are then placed on tables with tongs for attendees to pick up and put on plates given them by the same ladies, every year, ladies who grant each person that plate with a napkin, utensils and a smile. It may be 90, it may be 100 degrees or more, but the smiles never wane.

At the end of the pavilion, a marvelous contraption constructed by the late M.E. Argo, a machinist and Grady Lions Club member. He created the hush puppy machine back in the 1950s in his welding shop. Batter is fed into one end of the machine, which dribbles precise amounts into hot grease at the other. White-clad men in aprons with paddles in hand shepherd the pups down a trench, turning them, ensuring all achieve the perfect deep orangish-brown before they're swept up in a basket and deposited in a metal bowl, to be taken to stations out on the lawn. The hush puppies are sweet, savory and addictive.

The men who watch over the hush puppies, and many of those who pass through the crowds serving more fish, are actually prisoners from the Arkansas Department of Corrections, men who have received a day furlough and the promise of good eatin' in exchange for good behavior. The situation is beneficial to both the prisoners and to the Grady's Lions Club, the membership of which has dwindled over the years. Free labor in exchange for one of the most iconic feasts in the Arkansas Delta seems a fair trade.

The Grady Fish Fry is a must-stop for politicians running for state office, a yang to the yin of January's famed Gillett Coon Supper, and in an election year many will greet you as you enter and come sit with you to chat while you dine.

ICE CREAM

In Arkansas, ice cream means Yarnell's, the Searcy standard nearly lost to time when the Yarnell's family closed up shop in 2011. Re-opened less than a year later, those classic flavors dressed in the maroon and gold of company colors have returned to shelves with famed selections such as Ozark Black Walnut, Homemade Strawberry and Death by Chocolate. Yarnell's also provides specialty ice creams to restaurants, including the purple vanilla used at the Purple Cow restaurants in Little Rock, Hot Springs and Conway. It also makes a special Spark ice cream (a blue and gold tinted golden vanilla) served specifically at Spark Café inside Walton's 5 & 10, the Walmart Museum in Bentonville.

Locally sourced and made ice cream is also available at Loblolly Creamery in Little Rock, which produces its flavors from local items, with flavors such as lemon berry icebox pie, orange crème fraiche, cucumber cooler sorbet and Little Rock-y Road.

In Fayetteville, custom soft-serve is created and served by the folks at Burton's Creamery, which combines handmade soft serve ice cream with amusing and interesting flavors to create combinations such as the Elton John, The Duff and The Mint Condition.

Spark Ice Cream from Yarnell's on a cone at Spark Café in Bentonville.

Little Rock-It Pop scoop and a milkshake at Loblolly Creamery in Little Rock.

A Salty Dog at Burton's on Dickson in Fayetteville.

ITALIAN DINNERS

Pasta with tomato sauce is an Italian creation celebrated Arkansas-style. Several times a year, different Catholic parishes around the state sit down to dinner for fantastic spaghetti dinners.

The tradition of spaghetti dinners goes back to the immigrants who brought spaghetti

with them. They were Italian natives who came from an area around Rome in the last decade of the 19th century, who became American citizens and were located to Arkansas. Many came as part of a relocation funded by New York businessman Austin Corbin, to the Sunnyside Plantation near current-day Lake Village. These Italians arrived in the area between 1895 and 1897 and attempted to make a home for themselves in the muddy, humid Mississippi River alluvial plan. Many of them stayed in the area, while others traveled with Father Pietro Bandini to a new settlement in 1898 that became the community of Tontitown in northwest Arkansas (*see* Fried Chicken and Spaghetti).

These days, spaghetti suppers are celebrated by five of the state's venerated Catholic churches. The most famous of these is the Italian Dinner hosted over several nights at the Tontitown Grape Festival each August, at which the handmade spaghetti is served with Delta-style fried chicken over the course of several nights each August. The largest single dinner is held each October at St. Joseph's in Pine Bluff, where coleslaw is also served and where almost 700 gallons of sauce will be used. There's another that happens each October in the Pulaski County community of Little Italy. The oldest is the Our Lady of the Lake Luncheon, which has continued since 1909 in Lake Village. There's also the Catholic Point Picnic at Center Ridge, held by St. Joseph's Catholic Church, each June, where the sauce comes from parishioners who each make their own version at home and poured into the community pot for a truly unique flavor.

Tontitown Grape
Festival Italian Dinner.

ITALIAN ROAST

The creation of Kent Berry, this pork roast found at The Meat Shoppe in Gravel Ridge contains Italian seasonings, pepperoni, salami, provolone and mozzarella. Popular for holiday gatherings.

ITALIAN SALAD

A dressing-soaked salad traditionally served alongside fried chicken and spaghetti in the region around Tontitown. The salad is served each August as part of the Tontitown Grape Festival Italian dinners as well as restaurants The Venesian Inn and Mama Z's Cafe. *See also* Fried Chicken and Spaghetti *and* Italian Dinners.

Venesian Inn's Italian Salad

Garlic vinegar:
1 quart vinegar
2 Tablespoons powdered garlic

Salad:
1 cup garlic vinegar
2 heads lettuce
Salt
Granulated garlic
2 cups vegetable oil

Mix one quart vinegar with two tablespoons powdered garlic. Mix, cover and let stand two weeks. Thinly slice two heads of lettuce. Sprinkle lightly, to taste, with salt and granulated garlic. Combine one cup of the garlic vinegar with two cups oil. Add enough dressing to saturate lettuce. Mix thoroughly, the more the better. Serves six.

Italian salad at The Venesian Inn in Tontitown.

JACQUES & SUZANNE'S

The Restaurant Jacques et Suzanne was a coat-and-tie Swiss-French establishment on the thirtieth floor of the First National Bank Building (now the Regions Bank Building), opened in June 1975 by Swiss husband-wife restaurateurs Jacques and Suzanne Tritten. It was sold to Ed Moore of European Food Services a few months later. Original executive chef Paul Bash became the manager of general operations when the purchase was made; head waiter Louis Petit, from Belgium, bought in as part owner. Chef Denis Seyer joined the staff shortly after the opening.

The restaurant closed at the height of its popularity, on January 30, 1986. The chefs who came from its kitchens sparked (at this counting) some 30 restaurants that have shaped the flavor of Little Rock in the three decades hence.

In 2017, Continental Cuisine of Little Rock - the business group created by Bash, Moore, Petit and Seyer - became the initial inductee as proprietors into the Arkansas Food Hall of Fame. This recipe is from the *Benton Auxiliary Club Cookbook*.

Jacques & Suzanne's Vinaigrette Salad Sauce

1/2 small onion, chopped
5/8 cup tarragon vinegar,
   plus a few of the tarragon leaves
1 Tablespoon Dijon French mustard
1/2 teaspoon Worcestershire sauce
dash of Tabasco
1 large clove of garlic
fresh ground pepper

1 whole egg
2/3 cup olive oil
1 beef bouillon cube
3 Tablespoons boiling water
1 1/3 cup vegetable oil
   (corn or safflower)
salt to taste

Place chopped onion, vinegar, tarragon leaves, mustard, Worcestershire sauce, Tabasco, garlic, pepper and egg in blender and blend well. Slowly add the olive oil. Add the beef bouillon cube after it has been dissolved in the water and blend quickly. Blend in the salad oil, adding it in a gradual stream. Taste before adding salt. (Salad dressings should be a bit salty, because by the time the dressing is spread out over the leaves, the salty taste is dissipated.) Place dressing in covered jar and refrigerate, although the dressing will be more flavorful if not real cold when it is served. Dress salad greens at the last minute. Makes three cups of dressing.

JELLY

We love jelly in Arkansas, and we'll make almost anything out of it or with it. The smooth, sweet preparation of sugar and fruit tops our biscuits and toast, fills sandwiches and even some fried pies and is employed as a condiment that adds flavor and fruit to anything. It comes in all sorts of varieties, from blackberries to jalapeño peppers to wine must.

House of Webster in Rogers is a particularly popular purveyor of all things jelly. Started in 1934, this longtime Rogers standard offers jams, jellies, pickles and butters to the world along with world-class bacon, mixes and mustards. House of Webster was started by Roy and Evelynn Webster in 1934.

Just outside of Little Rock, Dennis and Linda Kolb run Bear Kingdom Vineyard, selling jams and jellies since 1995. The Kolbs grow their own jelly grapes, and also utilize juices and wines from Post Familie Vineyards in Altus in their products. Its most popular flavor, Cherub's Rapture, is a scrumptious combination of raspberry and cinnamon. All of the Kolbs' jellies are sugar-sweetened.

Ozark Mountain Jams in Huntsville has been operated by a Mennonite family since 2000. Their products, which include a large variety of jellies, jams and fruit butters, are available at many locations statewide.

JERKY

A long staple of settlers, cattlemen, hunters and fishing enthusiasts, spiced dried beef, venison, pork and other meats make for good shelf-stable snacking, whether it's for a trip into the woods or a day on the lake. You'll find jerky in almost any grocery or convenience store in Arkansas. In particular, you can find buffalo, elk and beef jerky from Ratchford Farms all over the state, and there's a special house jerky that's famed from Burl's Country Smokehouse.

Want to make your own? Here's a recipe from Cavender's.

Beef Jerky

1 bottle red wine
1 large bottle Heinz 57 sauce
1 large bottle teriyaki sauce
1 large bottle soy sauce
1 quart tomato juice

1 bottle worcestershire sauce
1/4 cup liquid smoke (maybe more)
1/2 cup Cavender's Greek Seasoning
2 Tablespoons garlic salt
20 lbs. beef, cut into strips.

Blend together all liquid ingredients and pour into large container. Place beef strips in liquid, making sure liquid gets in-between each strip. Soak for 24 hours. Lay strips out on heavy aluminum foil or oven racks. Sprinkle lightly with Cavender's Greek Seasoning and garlic salt. Dry for eight hours at 140 to 150 degrees or until completely dry. Store in a cool, dry place.

Beef jerky at Coursey's Smoked Meats in St. Joe.

JOHNNY CAKES or HOECAKES

A version of cornbread indigenous to the American South, this is a mixture of coarse cornmeal, water and salt, once cooked on a hoe greased with fatback over an open fire. Today's hoecakes are usually made in a greased cast iron skillet over high heat.

KEO KLASSIC

This standard on the menu at Charlotte's Eats and Sweets in Keo has few equals. The crust made by the Parmesan garlic batter on the grill is crispy, while the sourdough bread underneath is still white and fluffy, layers of Monterey Jack cheese, smoked turkey breast, tomato, white onion, avocado and more Monterey Jack elevate this simple dish to perfection. Remember to order your pie first when you go to Charlotte's - they usually run out of slices before the end of the day.

LEMONADE

The most famous lemonade ever found in Arkansas was that produced at Frank Brannan and Sons Drive-In in Conway. Brannan started out with Frank's Confectionery in 1939 before opening his eponymous drive-in on north Harkrider in 1945. The family kept the restaurant going until 1999; Frank's son Bobby took the famed foot longs and lemonade to several locations, including Julie's Sweet Shoppe, for trips down memory lane with his customers before his death in 2017.

LITTLE ROCK ROLL (noun)

The Japanese spots around Little Rock like to create their own version of this named roll. Sakura's includes fried shrimp, crab, lettuce, avocado, cucumber, tobiko and eel sauce; Mount Fuji's consists of boiled shrimp, avocado and cucumber, while Hanaroo's is cream cheese, crab stick, avocado, asparagus and potato salad fried and topped with chili sauce. There is at this time no consistent construction for the dish.

LITTLE ROCK ROLL (verb)

The action of dipping a tortilla chip in cheese dip, then rolling the chip back and forth so the excess ends up in the bowl instead of on your shirt.

Rolling excess cheese dip off a chip at Heights Taco and Tamale Co. in Little Rock.

MAMMOTH ORANGE CAFE

Ernestine Bradshaw opened the original round orange building in Redfield on June 1, 1965. She had lived in California before moving to Arkansas and was inspired to have a small dairy stand such as the many she'd seen there. Most of the orange stands she had found in California were either built by or inspired by the creations of Frank E. Pohl, who opened his first orange-shaped stand in 1926.

Singular in Arkansas, the Mammoth Orange Café eventually grew with the addition of a cinder block structure at its rear to accommodate dine-in customers. The original fare sold here was orange juice, ice cream and burgers.

Today, her grandson, Jock Carter, operates the facility. The menu has expanded to include hamburger steak with gravy, burgers and chicken sandwiches, catfish on Fridays and ice cream delights.

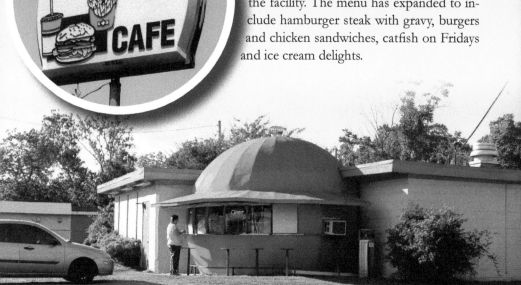

MASHED POTATOES

A common side dish around the state, mashed potatoes are the starch of choice in the northeastern portion of the Arkansas Delta, to the east of Crowley's Ridge. The sunken lands in the area are better suited for growing potatoes than state staple rice.

MEXICAN REGIONAL FOODS

Over the course of the past 30 years, southwest Little Rock has seen a demographic shift, with hundreds of Latino families making their homes in the area. The influx has also inspired a large number of restaurants featuring cuisine from

regions all across Mexico. For instance, Mariscos el Jarrocho features Gulf seafood dishes, while Taqueria Jalisco'z offers Pacific coast tacos and specialties. Bakeries, supermarkets and eateries representing several of Mexico's states have opened in the area. Similar trends have also been noted in Springdale and De Queen.

Above: Beef milanese torta at Eliella's Restaurant in Little Rock.
Below: Parriladda Jaliscoz at Taqueria Jalisco'z in Little Rock.

MAYHAW JELLY

The "southern cranberry" grows well in L.A. (Lower Arkansas), and it makes a strong and pungent jelly perfect for cathead biscuits. El Dorado even has a Mayhaw Festival each May. Paul's Mayhaw Orchard grows mayhaws and sells jelly made from the fruit.

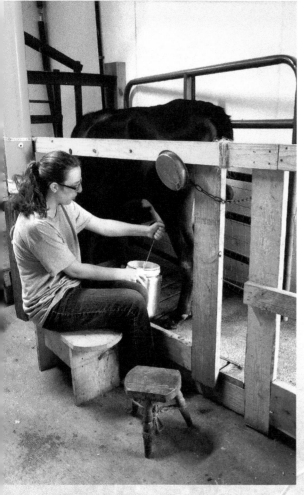

MILK

In 1985, milk was recognized as the official state beverage of Arkansas, for its healthfulness and because of the importance of the dairy sector in Arkansas. Milk and dairy products have been produced in Arkansas since early settlers' days. A bevy of Arkansas dairy producers once provided milk to communities all over the state. Today, much of the milk brought to market comes through Hiland Dairy.

In August 2013, legislation was signed allowing raw cow milk to legally be sold in Arkansas. The law allows for the sale of raw cow milk directly from the farm (not available for resale), with a limit of 500 gallons of raw cow milk and 500 gallons of raw goat milk each month.

In the Cozahome community just north of Harriet, Dogwood Hills Guest Farm allows individuals and families to come experience life on the farm, including the opportunity to milk the farm's resident cows. The facility also includes a Buttermilk Trail, where you can view the entire milk-making process from where the fodder is grown in a special barn to its eventual culinary application in buttermilk and cheese.

See also Cheese.

MILO

Long planted as a cover crop in rotation for farmers and used as feed for animals, grain sorghum or milo has recently made inroads as a human food crop here in Arkansas. We're third in the nation in grain sorghum production. Broom-corn, as it's also called, requires special cooking and has a unique, pearl-like texture. It's being explored as a gluten-free option for many chefs.

See also Sorghum Molasses.

MINUTE MAN

What would Wendy's be like without the slogan "Old-Fashioned Hamburgers?" Would fast food restaurants be the same without product give-aways? And would those chains be so popular without special meals for kids? These sort of developments were part of the marketing genius of an Arkansas-based hamburger chain that's almost faded from history - Minute Man.

Wes Hall's original concept restaurant came out of a 24-hour coffee shop he owned with two other partners at 407 Broadway in Little Rock back in 1948. Eight years into the operation, he bought out his partners and converted the place into a hamburger joint. Soon, he had franchised out the Minute Man name and product across the state and even further – to seven states and 57 locations.

Hall's first restaurant was one of three in the nation to receive brand new micro-wave "Radar Ranges" from Raytheon to try out – and Minute Man pioneered microwave usage in fast food. If you ever had the chance to savor a Radar Deep Dish Pie (if you were smart enough to let it cool, of course, and didn't singe off your taste buds), you had a microwaved food item – a disc of doughy crust atop the bubbling magma of filling – in cherry, peach, apple or strawberry.

He understood marketing before marketing was a thing in Arkansas. He figured out what people wanted and got them to buy those things from his store. And he knew how to cross-promote. Back in 1975, he teamed up with the Coca-Cola company to do something revolutionary – offer a real glass with the Minute Man logo with a drink purchase. You'll still see those bold red, white and blue bi-centennial glasses in homes and on the shelves of local flea markets.

1975 was also the year the Magic Meal was patented. It may be hard for some of you younger folks to believe, but used to be if you wanted to order something for your kid, it came off the same menu as the adults used. The patent includes word-

ing such as "PREPARING A HAMBURGER SANDWICH WITH FRENCH FRIED POTATOES SOLD IN A SPECIAL CONTAINER WHICH CONTAINS A MAGIC TRICK, SOLD AS PART OF A RESTAURANT OPERATION." Minute Man sold Magic Meals two years before McDonald's recognizes the birth of the Happy Meal. Eventually Minute Man sold the rights to sell Magic Meals (including the name) to Burger King – which offered them first in 1982.

Minute Man also beat McDonald's to the punch on a signature sandwich. The "Big M" was a double full-sized patty burger that came with cheese, chopped onion, lettuce, tomato and a relish sauce which debuted in 1966. The Big Mac, McDonald's signature burger, debuted in 1967 at a single location in Pennsylvania.

Over the years, there have been rumors for years that the Minute Man chain could be franchised out, but as of this writing it's still all but naught. Still, for those of us who have missed relish sauce and such, there is a single location of the Minute Man left. It's in El Dorado on Main Street, a few blocks from the downtown square, which has that relish sauce and is in one of the original Minute Man buildings.

Joe St. Columbia, the grandson of the original Arkansas Delta Tamale creator, sent me a recipe a few years ago. I opened that envelope expecting a tamale recipe. Instead, it contained the coveted sauce recipe from Minute Man – the special sauce that preceded McDonald's Special Sauce. It came on a #1 burger with lettuce, tomato and onion. And now, you can recreate it yourself.

Minute Man Special Sauce

1-28 ounce bottle ketchup	1 Tablespoon sugar
1-12 ounce bottle chili sauce	1 teaspoon liquid smoke
1-28 ounce can stewed tomatoes, pureed	Salt and pepper to taste

Mix ketchup, chili sauce, stewed tomatoes and sugar and simmer over low heat until thick. Add liquid smoke to taste and serve over hamburgers as a tasty sauce. Serves 25.

MISTA SALAD

The house salad at Lazzari Italian Oven in Jonesboro, this tossed salad of lettuce, tomato, pepperoncinis, black olives and mozzarella cheese comes drizzled in a sweet, lightly peppery vinaigrette. A special treat for Arkansas State University students and fellow diners since 1995.

MIXERS

pink House alchemy (yes, only the H is capitalized) offers a variety of mixers that offer that extra special something to create an extraordinary version of any mixed drink. The Fayetteville operation aims at finding the connections between foods and flavors to conjure original and delectable syrups (which add sweetness), bitters (which add pungent flavors) and shrubs (which add acidity) for beverages.

MONK SAUCE

Father Richard Walz brought back Habanero pepper seeds from his tenure in Belize, and planted them at the monastery at Subiaco. In 2003, Monk Sauce hit the market. The significant heat in these sauces comes from the extra time and care spent with the peppers.

MONTE NE INN CHICKEN RESTAURANT

The restaurant outside of Rogers in the Monte Ne community is one of the few places in Arkansas where you can still sit down and break bread with your family over a communally shared dinner. It starts with a pot of white bean soup in a bean pot, and continues with fresh baked bread, apple butter, corn, mashed potatoes, gravy, coleslaw and some of the best fried chicken in the state. Dessert is extra.

MOUNTAINBURGER

Arkansas's only loosemeat burger is offered at the Dairy Dream, a walk-up dairy bar along the Boston Mountain Loop in Mountainburg. The restaurant has offered these unusual burgers, which have the consistency of a Sloppy Joe, to customers since it opened in 1954. The loose ground meat in its minimal sauce is served with your choice of cheese, pickle, mustard and onion.

The Dairy Dream also offers so many flavors of the past in its drink selection, with Silver Saddles, Purple Cows, Red Rovers, Baby Elephants and Wildcats. The eatery also offers the tallest soft serve cones in that neck of the woods.

MOUNTAIN VALLEY WATER

Back in the 19th century, Benjamin Lockett and his son Enoch started bottling the water from a spring on their land just outside of Hot Springs. Lockett's Spring Water was acquired in 1871 by Peter and John Greene, who renamed the precious resource by the name it bears today - Mountain Valley Water. The Greenes sold the land and the water to W. N. Benton in 1879. He in turn marketed it as a cure-all, founding the Mountain Valley Water Company with Zeb Ward, G. G. Latta, Samuel Stitt and Samuel Fordyce (for whom the Fordyce Bathhouse is named) in 1883. Nine years later, Ward bought out his partners. In 1894, Mountain Valley Water Company opened its first franchise in Philadelphia.

The Swiss immigrant August Schlafly purchased the company in 1897. Under his tenure the company expanded to Chicago and New York. By the 1920s, Mountain Valley Water was being served in the United States Senate. In 1928, another franchise was created in California, making Mountain Valley Water available coast to coast.

Not only a delicious, clear water from a babbling spring, this particular water was credited with curing kidney and liver ailments as well as dyspepsia, dropsy, and Bright's Disease. The company founded to promote the beverage created one of the first nationwide franchises in America, and continues to offer the original water today, along with sparkling and flavored versions.

August Schlafly purchased the DeSoto Springs Mineral Water Company, a competitor, in 1924. The Classical Revival building was renovated and a third story Japanese-themed dance hall was added. The DeSoto Spring Water Depot and Dance Hall would continue to operate until 1936, when the headquarters for Mountain Valley Water were moved to this location, creating a visitors center on Central Avenue still open today.

MUSCADINES

Indigenous to Arkansas, these wild grapes have a thick skin most people spit out. They've been cultivated since the 16th century in the southeastern portion of the United States. Muscadines make great jelly. They also make an excellent juice and wine. Both Post Familie and Wiederkehr Wine Cellars offer muscadine wine and juice for sale. Green muscadines are known as scuppernongs.

To find a wild muscadine vine, look along country roadsides - they are still found across much of the state. To eat a muscadine, one usually bites a hole in the skin and sucks out the juice, spitting out the seed.

This wine recipe comes from a cookbook from the *Kommon Cents Kookin' Club of Hot Springs, Arkansas* (1978), and is attributed to Terry Adams.

Muscadine Wine

½ bushel muscadines
12 ½ lbs. sugar

Mash the muscadine grapes with your hands. Put them in a large churn and add 2 ½ pounds sugar and let it work (ferment for about one week until it quits bubbling). Strain the mixture to get out grape skins and impurities. Put back in churn and add 10 pounds sugar. Let it work about eight to 10 days until it quits fermenting. Makes about four gallons.

MUSHROOMS

The fleshy, spore-bearing fruiting body of a fungus, typically produced above ground on soil or on its food source. More than 200 different sorts of mushroom have been identified in Arkansas as native species. Not all are edible - some are downright poisonous. Amongst edible favorites, you'll find the Arkansas Silver Caesar, Bolete, Morel, Chanterelle and multiple varieties known as "chicken of the woods." Many farmers' cooperatives now sell Arkansas-raised and found mushrooms. Please take care to examine and identify before consumption.

THE NUTTY BIRD

Served at Izzy's, a popular restaurant in West Little Rock, this sandwich is sliced turkey breast, cream cheese, sunflower seeds, leaf lettuce, tomato and Miracle Whip, on natural grain bread. Izzy's is also known for its marvelous selection of loose leaf teas and its honey, gathered from its own on-site apiary.

THE NUTTY BUDDY

Opened in 1971, King Kone in Hot Springs offers a homemade Nutty Buddy ice cream cone. Unlike its tiny namesake, this dairy bar constructs its version in a housemade waffle cone, filled with soft serve vanilla ice cream and chopped peanuts, dipped in magic chocolate shell.

OATS

One of Arkansas's primary winter grains, grown over the fall and harvested in May or June. Oats are primarily grown for seed here in Arkansas, where most of the crop is shipped to Texas.

That being said, oats and oatmeal are a part of the Arkansas diet. Organic steel cut and rolled oats can be purchased from War Eagle Mill. If you're looking for an incredible oatmeal cookie, order one with your cuppa at Mylo Coffee Company in Little Rock's Hillcrest District.

OKRA

This misunderstood vegetable has roots in both central Asia and northern Africa, particularly Ethiopia. It's a member of the mallow family, like cotton and hibiscus. In the South, it has long been a subject of debate for its optional application in gumbo, but few would argue its place as a side dish when fried. Most folks fry it in slices, though Donnie Ferneau at Little Rock's Cathead's Diner chooses to fry it whole. It can also be found pickled at Elizabeth's in Batesville. Multi-James Beard Award nominated Chef Matthew McClure of The Hive at 21c in Bentonville shares this recipe for a gorgeously stewed Okratouille.

Okratouille

1 yellow onion, diced	Aleppo pepper
1 pint chopped tomatoes	salt
1 cup summer squash, diced	canola oil
1 pint fresh okra, sliced 1/2-inch thick	

Stew the onion with oil and salt until translucent. Add chopped tomato to onions and continue to stew until they are completely cooked through and tender.

In a cast iron pan, begin to sear squash and okra over medium-high heat in canola oil; do not overcook. Allow the squash to cook until it is golden-brown but not mushy. Repeat this process until all of the squash and okra are cooked and added to the stew.

Once the stew is built, simmer over low heat for 20 minutes to allow the flavors to blend and to thoroughly cook the okra. Finish with a generous pinch of Aleppa pepper. Taste and adjust seasoning as desired.

FRIED OKRA

1/2 pound fresh okra
1/4 teaspoon salt
Pinch ground black pepper
1 Tablespoon water
3/4 cup fine-ground
    white cornmeal
1 Tablespoon cornstarch
Oil for frying

Rinse and drain okra, then
cut the tips and tops off
and slice crosswise into 1/3"
rounds. Put sliced okra in a
mixing bowl and season lightly
with salt and pepper. Sprinkle over
the water and toss to evenly mix.

Whisk together the cornmeal, cornstarch, salt
and black pepper. Heat three inches of oil in a heavy pot to 350 F.

When the oil is heated, toss the sliced and seasoned okra in the cornmeal mixture.
Coat evenly and shake gently in a sieve to remove any extra dredge. Fry in the hot
oil until lightly golden brown, about 5 minutes. Drain well.

OLD FASHIONED CHOCOLATE FRIED PIES

This particular variant on the fried pie includes a filling of flour, sugar and butter that dates back a century. So far, I've only found them sold commercially at Batten's Bakery in Paragould and at Snappy Food Marts in Damascus and Bee Branch. They're a favorite that I've enjoyed since I was a kid.

Old Fashioned Chocolate Fried Pies

1/2 cup sugar
1/4 cup flour
1 Tablespoon unsweetened cocoa powder
1/2 cup milk
2 Tablespoons butter

1/2 teaspoon vanilla
2 cups biscuit mix
1/2 cup milk
cooking oil (for frying)
sifted powdered sugar

In a saucepan combine sugar, flour, and unsweetened cocoa powder. Stir in 1/2 cup milk and butter or margarine. Cook over medium heat till the mixture is thickened and bubbly. Stir constantly. Stir in vanilla. Cool.

In a mixing bowl stir together the biscuit mix and 1/2 cup milk. On a well-floured surface, knead the dough 12 times. Roll the dough to 1/8 inch thickness. Cut dough into twelve inch circles.

Place one tablespoon filling in the center of each circle of dough. Brush the edge of the dough with water. Fold the dough over the filling; press the edges together with tines of a fork to seal.

In a skillet heat one inch cooking oil to 375 degrees. Fry the pastries for about two minutes, or until golden. Turn once. Drain on paper towel and sprinkle warm pastries with sifted powdered sugar.

The OLD SOUTH

The Old South, a classic eatery still operating in Russellville, was built in 1947, a couple of years after the end of the second World War. It wasn't the first. That was The Old South in Fort Smith... opened around 1945 at 711 Towson Avenue (now a parking lot for Sparks Regional Medical Center). Confused?

The Old South was a concept restaurant – a franchise created as a turnkey operation. William E. Stell, an Oklahoma-born businessman who created and founded the National Glass and Manufacturing Company in Fort Smith back in 1929, came up with the idea. The company created fixtures, furniture and metalwork for restaurants and department stores. Stell decided to develop a modular diner system. Unlike the Streamliner design (which was a contained prefab unit), Stell's idea was for a modular build-on-site system that could be adapted to the location. He employed the help of architect Glenn Pendergrass (he designed the El Chico restaurants around Dallas) to design the concept he envisioned. The first, that Fort Smith store, was an experiment. Stell brought R. C. Strub of Schwab's in from New York City to form a Kansas City-style steakhouse menu for the chain.

The last week of March, 1947, Stell delivered on a contract to Woody Mays, owner of Woody's Classic Inn and Coffee Shop, and had this Russellville location built in just six days. It opened on April 4th, 1947. It was added to the National Historic Register in 1999, for its definitive construction and its significance as a favorite road travel stop for B.B. King, Ernest Tubbs and Elvis Presley. Though there were once dozens of The Old South restaurants across the United States, this is the last one. Here's the recipe for the restaurant's famed dressing.

Old South Garlic Salad Dressing

2 ounces Bleu cheese
1/4 cup salad olives in brine

2 Tablespoons garlic powder
1 quart Kraft REAL Mayonnaise

Blend the first three ingredients together in a food processor until incorporated. Add mayo and blend until smooth. Store in refrigerator for up to three months.

A mess of onion rings at Hoot's BBQ in McGehee.

ONION RINGS

The first instance of battered and fried onions known came from John Mollard's *The Art of Cookery Made Easy and Refined*, published in 1802. In his recipe "Fried Onions with Parmezan Cheese," Mollard calls for cutting onions into 1/2" rings, dipping them into a batter made of flour, cream, salt, pepper, and Parmesan, then deep frying them in boiling lard. Much has changed since those days, but onion rings are decidedly a part of our culinary lexicon. Lots of great varieties are available around the state, including these at Hoot's BBQ in McGehee.

OX TAILS

The tail of a cow, skinned and butchered, ox tails are simmered for hours or even pressure cooked to properly disperse gelatin in the meat. The uncooked ox tail is usually two to four pounds and is cut into rounds by a butcher. This soul food classic is often a lunch special at restaurants such as David Family Kitchen in Little Rock. In the past decade, more upscale restaurants looking to return to Southern roots have added it to seasonal menus.

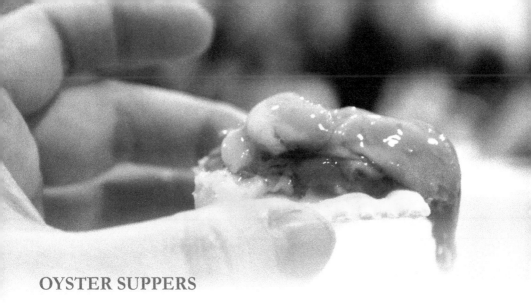

OYSTER SUPPERS

In the winter, groups around the state hold a variety of dinners and breakfasts to fund everything from scholarships to community projects. Among them are two oyster suppers – one held in January by the Knights of Columbus in Slovak, and one held in February by the McGehee Men's Club in McGehee.

The latter started in 1995 with just 200 people in attendance, and has worked its way up to a 1200+ person event. The proceeds go to several organizations and to funding an annual scholarship program. Each year, members of the Men's Club take a couple of trucks with chest freezers down to the Gulf Coast, purchase oysters straight off the boat and drive them back to McGehee to be served fresh, raw and fried, to a crowd of men, women and children who come from all over for the celebration. The oysters are paired with fried catfish, crinkle cut fries, Italian soaked salad and hush puppies, along with cocktail sauce and saltines for your oysters.

OZARKIES

A Kopper Kettle Candies specialty delight - a light vanilla cream center covered with rich milk chocolate, dark vanilla chocolate and pecans.

PANCAKES

A breakfast staple that utilizes a flour-based batter poured onto a hot griddle or skillet, traditionally served with maple syrup or maple-flavored corn syrup. The relatively cheap ingredients and quick speed of cooking makes this a perfect item for any breakfast.

The Pancake Shop in Hot Springs is one of the longest running purveyors of the staple, serving plate-sized versions in buckwheat, blueberry, banana, apple and traditional varieties. Open since 1940, the waitresses still call you "honey" and, thanks to a gigantic antique gas-heated urn, the coffee is the hottest in the city. The mix for the legendary pancakes is offered next door at Savory Pantry.

Benson's Grill in Fort Smith offers a special version with sweet potatoes that goes remarkably well with syrup. New startup Prelude Breakfast Bar in Fayetteville delights in its Pancake Flights, which give you the opportunity to sample three smaller pancakes with different flavors and fillings.

You can even order organic pancake mix in several varieties, including multi-grain, pecan cinnamon whole grain, buckwheat, and blue cornmeal, from War Eagle Mill. The Bean Palace atop the mill offers these pancakes daily for breakfast, and on a breakfast buffet bar each Saturday and Sunday.

PAN FRIED POTATOES

Skillet fried potatoes are pretty common all across Arkansas. They have long been more common than shredded hashbrowns for breakfast or French fries for dinner. Their simplicity comes in the ingredients - two items that grow easily in a garden, that are cheap and that keep for a long time in the larder, cooked in the grease of whatever meat has been in the skillet last, seasoned with just table salt and black pepper. Fancier versions have become common, but the five elements - potatoes, onion, salt, pepper and fat - are all you really need. Here's what I serve.

A skillet's worth of potatoes cut
   into 1-2 inch chunks
   (I like Yukon Gold)

1 onion, diced
2 Tablespoons butter
Salt and pepper to taste

Melt butter in skillet over high heat. Add onions and fry, continually stirring, until translucent. Add potatoes and stir until coated in butter, then reduce heat and cover, stirring occasionally, until potatoes are tender Salt and pepper to taste.

PARADISE PIE

A rich, expensive-tasting pie made from saltine crackers, cream and coconut. The most famous example was created by Ruby Thomas at the Red Apple Inn in Heber Springs. The delectable dish is still served today, despite humble origins as a Depression-era pie.

PASTA

Arkansas's considerable Italian immigrant population continues several culinary traditions of their homeland that involve sauces, soaked salads and pasta.

Each year for the Tontitown Grape Festival, volunteers make 3000 pounds of spaghetti over the course of two weeks in July. It's paired up with homemade sauce and served to nearly 10,000 people during four nights of the festival each August.

Pozza's Pasta, which has been in business for almost 40 years, still uses recipes from the original Tontitown settlers in its original, handmade and dried pastas. Lucius and Alison Mhoon purchased the company in 2005 and continue the original traditions. This recipe for pasta sauce is shared on the Pozza's Pasta website.

Pozza's Pasta Sauce

2 lbs. lean ground beef
3 6-ounce cans tomato paste
3 sticks celery
1 medium onion
3 garlic buds (cloves)
Salt and pepper to taste

1 stick butter
3 cups water

Chop fine or blend in blender parsley, onion and garlic. Sauté in butter 15 minutes. Add meat and brown. Add tomato paste and water, salt and pepper and stir well. Simmer uncovered at low heat for four to five hours or more, or bake uncovered at 225 degrees for four hours or more.

**Spaghetti and meatballs at
The Venesian Inn in Tontitown.**

PAW PAWS

Amsonia triloba is an understory tree that grows 10 to 15 feet tall, which belongs to the tropical custard apple family. Its tangy-banana-ish flavor has been savored for ages here in Arkansas; the fruit is one of the oldest fruits native to North America. It's sometimes called the Ozark banana.

Scott Bauer - USDA

Paw paws are generally green in color with a creamy inside. You can eat the creamy part, but the seeds and the skin cause severe indigestion – and the flesh must be entirely ripe. The fruit lasts less than a week in refrigeration, so unless you know someone with a tree, you're not likely to find them. They can be eaten raw, baked or even in pie, where the pineapple-banana flavor pairs well with cream.

PCP

A popular pie at Ed and Kay's in Benton, a restaurant open for more than 50 years which closed in 2015. This baked pie includes pineapple, coconut and pecan on a traditional crust. A similar pie was once offered at The Station Restaurant in Pine Bluff. This recipe is from *A Great Taste of Arkansas: A Recipe Collection* (1986).

Pineapple Coconut Pecan Pie

¼ cup butter
2 cups sugar
4 eggs
1 ½ cup (7 ounce package) coconut

½ cup pecans
6 ounces crushed pineapple, drained
Unbaked 9" pie shell.

Cream butter and sugar. Add eggs and blend in coconut, nuts and pineapple. Pour into unbaked pie shell and bake at 350 degrees until firm, about one hour.

PEACHES

There's nothing quite like a fresh, dripping bite of a peach in the middle of summer. While you can acquire them at the store or pick them up at the farmer's market, little beats picking one straight off a tree.

Peaches weren't cultivated in Arkansas until after the Civil War. As farmers diversified crops to avoid the treacheries of a single crop economy, orchards popped up in central and western Arkansas and along Crowley's Ridge. These peaches were juicy but they didn't have a long shelf life, so any fruit that traveled far for market tended to go to mush. The introduction of the Elberta peach, cultivated by Samuel Rumph of Georgia (and named for his wife) in 1879 made the fruit more viable as a commodity. His yellow-fleshed orb was firmer and ripened more slowly than other varieties, allowing pecks and bushels to be shipped away from the immediate area. The introduction of refrigerated rail shipping expanded the market, and peach farming took firm hold.

In Johnson County, peaches have been big business for over a century. Johnson Taylor and James Tolbert began growing Elberta peaches in 1893, and others followed suit. In 1897, the Missouri Pacific Railroad partnered with the area's peach farmers to ship local fruit. Ten boxcar loads of peaches left the western Arkansas county each year by 1901, and a couple hundred thousand bushels were produced throughout the state by the 1910s. Though disasters took their toll in the 1950s, the peach is still recognized as an Arkansas favorite.

The Morgan family has been working with peaches for five generations at Peach Pickin' Paradise, just outside of Lamar. The orchard has been carefully managed to produce 20 varieties, some which mature early, others late, to ensure there are peaches for the public to pick from the first of July to the end of August.

More than a dozen other peach orchards are open to the public during July and August, depending on when the harvest comes in. Johnson County celebrates the peach annually with Arkansas's oldest food festival, each July in Clarksville.

An older recipe from my family for peach preserves creates almost candied, translucent peach slices which fit perfectly on a biscuit.

Peach Preserves

Two dozen ripe peaches
4 oranges
8 cups sugar

Peel and slice peaches into 1/8 inch rounds. Place in airtight container. Slice oranges (without peeling them) into similar rounds and lay over top. Pour over sugar and tightly seal. Refrigerate overnight.

In a heavy pot, simmer slowly until liquid thickens and peaches become transparent. Keep stirring to prevent sticking. Layer peach slices into jars, reserving orange slices for other uses. Pour remaining liquid over slices. Seal.

PEANUT BUTTER

Skippy Foods has produced peanut butter in Little Rock since 1977. Eleven varieties of peanut butter are made at the plant on the east side of town. Every day, approximately 750,000 pounds of peanuts are brought in for processing to make the company's 11 varieties. More than three and a half million pounds of peanut butter are made at the facility each year.

PEANUTS

The goobers in our fields are the 10th largest crop in the state of Arkansas. That's quite a bit of change. As recently as 2010, there were just 560 acres of peanuts planted in The Natural State; that number increased to 30,000 in 2017. Most of those fields are concentrated in the northeast Delta in Randolph, Craighead, Mississippi and Lawrence counties.

Planters Peanuts are processed for a variety of products in Fort Smith, one of two locations for the company. The other is in Suffolk, Virginia.

Peanut butter pie at Three Sams BBQ Joint in Mabelvale.

PEANUT BUTTER PIE

Vincent Price was well known for his acting career. He was in more than 100 movies that crossed genres, but he's probably best known for his horror roles. Price was also a gourmet cook and pie lover – and when he dined at Sue's Kitchen in Jonesboro back in the early 1980s, he fell in love with a particular pie and actually talked Sue Williams out of the recipe.

This recipe for peanut butter pie comes from a different Sue, one by the name of Sue Hanebrink in the 1978 cookbook *Sue's Kitchens*.

Peanut Butter Pie

2/3 cup sugar
3 Tablespoons cornstarch
  or 5 Tablespoons flour
½ teaspoon salt

2 ½ cups milk
3 egg yolks, beaten
1 teaspoon vanilla
3 Tablespoons peanut butter

Combine sugar and cornstarch or flour and salt in top of a double boiler. Stir in cold milk. Cook over boiling water until thickened, stirring constantly. Cover and cook 15 minutes.

Stir a little hot mixture into beaten yolks, add to mixture in double boiler and cook for two minutes over hot, not boiling, water, stirring. Remove from heat, stir in peanut butter. Cool, add vanilla.

Pour into baked pie shell and add topping.

Topping:

½ cup cold milk
½ teaspoon vanilla
2 Tablespoons peanut butter

2 Tablespoons sugar
1 package Dream Whip

Blend at high speed until peaks form.

PEANUT PATTIES

These delightful sugary creations that have often graced the palm or pocket of a traveler in need of sweet delights, are common in the southwest. Peanuts are boiled in a pot together with corn syrup, sugar and other ingredients to create a candy, which is poured into molds and allowed to set. While you can find peanut patties around the state at convenience stores, they are predominantly a south-west Arkansas confection.

Elve Otwell created the Elve's Candy Company in Texarkana 1956, after working for another company that made peanut patties. His pinkish patties became a staple in Miller County. Today, Joe and Shelly Hickey own the company, and keep the Elve's tradition alive, making the patties by the original recipe. Elve's patties are different from other peanut patties because they utilize absolutely no food coloring – the color of the patty comes from the skins of the peanuts.

The recipe for Elve's peanut patties is a secret. This recipe, found in *Arkansas Country Cooking: Original Arkansas Recipes* (1981, compiled by Faye Crews of Murfreesboro), utilizes several ingredients not found in the Elve's version.

Peanut Patties

2 ½ cups sugar
2/3 cup white Karo syrup
2 ½ cups raw peanuts
1 cup milk

4 teaspoons margarine
1 cup powdered sugar
Few drops of red food coloring
   (optional)

Combine sugar, syrup, peanuts and milk and cook slowly in large pan until it forms a soft ball in cold water. Remove from heat and add remaining ingredients. Stir until it begins to thicken. Drop by tablespoonfulls on wax paper. Leave it at room temperature until it cools. Each spoonful will spread.

PEARS

Not quite as widespread as apples, you'll still find some pear orchards here and there in Arkansas. Quite a few varieties are grown here, such as Moonglow, Seckel and Comice. Maybe it's something particular to my family, but pears have always been part of my Arkansas experience. I remember the hard pears on the trees at the end of summer and the pear preserves on biscuits, and pear mincemeat pie during the holidays.

Pear Mincemeat for Pie Filling

7 pounds pears, pared and sliced
12 apples, pared and sliced
3 oranges, peeled and sectioned
2 pounds raisins
1 ½ cups brown sugar
5 cups sugar
½ cup white vinegar
1 Tablespoon cloves
1 Tablespoon nutmeg
1 Tablespoon cinnamon

Combine all ingredients in pot over high heat. Boil for three minutes, stirring constantly. Seal in jars or freeze.

U.S. Department of Agriculture Pomological Watercolor Collection

PECANS

Indigenous to Arkansas, pecans make a welcome late-fall protein addition that appears in everything from pie to casseroles. They're also great for snacking.

Pecans were highly valued by Native Americans, who traded and consumed them. Spanish explorers thought they were a sort of walnut and called them nueces, or "fruit of the walnut." They're a great source of protein, and somewhat easier to crack than walnuts.

In our nascent days of road travel, when the automobile was first looked at as a means to explore and enjoy the world on vacation, roadside stands popped up offering shelled and roasted pecans to take home. That tradition continues with Ozark Nut Roasters, based in North Little Rock, which not only roasts pecans but sells them in coated varieties such as cinnamon roasted, praline, and milk chocolate-covered.

November is when you may find many rural Arkansawyers bent over in the country, looking at the ground. No contacts have been lost. These are simply individuals doing the good work of picking up pecans.

Each year, an estimated 2.6 million pecans are harvested from orchards around Arkansas. In places such as Keo, where pecan groves are common, the harvest is a community event. Keo even has a tree-shaker to get those nuts down to the earth. Arkansas pecans can be picked up in-season from Me and McGee Market in North Little Rock, Burgener's Pecans in Hot Springs, Smith Pecan House in Helena-West Helena, and Foshee Pecans in Blackwell, among others.

Pecans are a very popular ingredient in pies of all sorts across Arkansas, from the traditional pecan pie to several varieties of chocolate bourbon pecan to peach-pecan. They're even the key ingredient in the crust and topping for possum pie. Pecans can also be found in sweet potato casseroles, mixed into the cranberry relish and sometimes even included in a good cornmeal dressing (*see* Cornbread Dressing *for recipe*).

PECAN JOE

PECAN JOE'S·FINE CANDIES · SOUVENIRS·OZARK HAMS·PRALINES·

But pecans aren't just for the holidays. You'll find them embedded in pancakes at War Eagle Mill's Bean Palace Restaurant, in waffles at Lewis Family Restaurant in Fort Smith, and encased in Juanita's pecan brittle. They're at the heart of fudge and Turtles at PattiCakes Bakery in Conway, and the nutty base for Wicked Mix (*see* Wicked Mix).

PECAN PIE

It should come as no surprise that we like our pecans in pie. The tradition of Karo pie goes back more than a century. We love our pecans in other sorts of amalgamations, from pecan cream cheese pie to bourbon chocolate pecan pies. Every region in the state boasts several pecan pie options.

Brown Sugar Pecan Pie

2 eggs, beaten
2 sticks (1/2 pound) butter, melted
1 cup light brown sugar
1/4 cup sugar (the white stuff)
1 teaspoon vanilla

1 Tablespoon all-purpose flour
1 cup chopped pecans
1/2 cup pecan halves
1 blind baked flour pastry pie shell
   (store-bought is acceptable, too)

Heat oven to 350 degrees.

Beat the heck out of the eggs. Pour in the melted butter, both sugars and the vanilla and incorporate thoroughly. Shake chopped pecans with all-purpose flour and add to the mix.

Pour into pie shell. Top with pecan halves. Bake for 45 minutes or until inserted toothpick comes out clean.

Caramel pecan pie at Fork and Crust in Rogers.

PECK SALAD

The great Little Rock hotels of the early 20th century included the venerable Hotel Sam Peck, located downtown and fondly remembered. One favored dish from that hotel, the Peck Salad, is still served at Capi Peck's celebrated Trio's Restaurant. Shredded chicken, bacon, slivered almonds and sweet vinaigrette over ripped romaine and leaf lettuce, the beloved salad has fans everywhere.

PEPPER JELLY

Pepper jelly is used as a condiment and as an appetizer, sometimes even as a component in congealed salads. Many Arkansas jellymakers, including Ozark Country Market in Heber Springs and House of Webster in Rogers, offer it. Off the Rails Jalapeño Jellies are a new favorite, in flavors such as pineapple mango, strawberry basil and cranberry orange. The simplest recipe utilizing pepper jelly? Open a block of cream cheese and pour pepper jelly over it. Serve with crackers. Sometimes I get fancy and mold my cream cheese first. The combination of sweet heat and dairy goes over well - and makes the ultimate "I forgot to cook, what can I bring to this party?" appetizer.

PEPPERED BACON

Brown sugar and pepper-coated bacon has been made by the Ruff Family, which owns Petit Jean Meats, for more than 60 years. Each slab is cured in a "family secret" wet brine of salt, sugar and spices for four or five days. It's smoked over hickory for just under 24 hours, rolled in brown sugar and finally hand-rubbed with cracked black peppercorns. Get yours at Petit Jean Meats in Morrilton.

PEPPERS

Both sweet and hot peppers grow well in Arkansas. Peppers originate in Central and South America back to antiquity. Arkansas's four-season state status makes for good pepper growing. Jalapeño, serrano and Hungarian wax cultivars are common, as are banana peppers and a whole range of sweet bells.

PHÓ

A Vietnamese soup consisting of broth, noodles, vegetables and protein, phó has developed a strong following - especially in Fort Smith, where Vietnamese descendants that came through Fort Chaffee in the 1970s have made their home. The town is home to a host of phó restaurants, each with its own specialties. Over the course of the second decade of the 21st century, that love has spread, and phó restaurants have now appeared in central and northeast Arkansas as well.

PICKLED EGGS

Present on the counter at old country stores and gas stations all over rural Arkansas, these preserved boiled eggs are a burst of spicy, salty protein that's easy to consume on a fishing trip or a day out hunting. Preserving eggs is nothing new – many cultures have done this for centuries. While you can find many varieties of pickled eggs commercially, home versions and recipes exist, including curried eggs, dilled eggs, and the bright red pickled eggs.

This recipe comes from *Arkansas Cookin',* compiled by Jean Wade in 1975.

Heber Springs Pickled Eggs

1 medium onion, sliced
1 ¾ cups white vinegar
¾ cups water
3 Tablespoons brown sugar
½ teaspoon salt
¼ teaspoon garlic salt

5 peppercorns
1 whole clove
¼ teaspoon dill seed
Red food coloring (optional)
18 hard-cooked eggs

Combine first nine ingredients, bring to a boil. Simmer for five minute; add desired amount of food coloring. Pour over eggs; cool. Refrigerate overnight. Will keep for two weeks.

This recipe comes from *Cooking with Pope County Extension Homemakers* (2000), one of the many cookbooks in my personal collection.

Red Beet Eggs

1 can beets
½ cup cider vinegar
¼ cup sugar

1 dozen boiled eggs
½ cup water
¼ teaspoon salt

Boil eggs in shell; set aside. Mix remaining ingredients together and heat to boiling. Put eggs in bowl or large glass jar and pour hot beets and juice over them. Refrigerate. Best left overnight.

PICKLED VEGETABLES

Few Arkansas vegetables avoid brining. You'll find everything from cabbage to carrots canned with vinegar and spices for keeping. You can also purchase pickled vegetables from Arkansas vendors, such as the Amish and Country Store near Dermott. Bryant Preserving Company of Alma produces jars of Old South pickled vegetables, from baby corn to watermelon rind, Brussels sprouts to garlic.

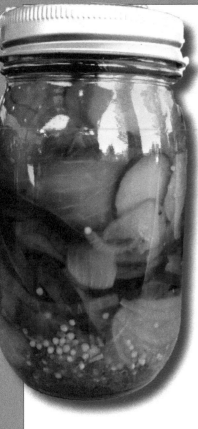

PICKLES

Atkins was once noted as the Pickle Capital of the World. Its main export, up to the 1990s, was pickles from the Atkins Pickle Company. The company opened its doors in 1946, originally taking on 100 employees but quickly adding 50 more. In 1951, chemist Robert Switzer was hired to create many of the particular flavors and blends of pickles offered at the plant (*see also* Tomolives). Working with 821 contracted farmers, Atkins Pickle Company would take in more than 1200 acres of cucumbers a year, providing a great source of employment for the town and inspiration for one of our home-grown dishes (*see* Fried Pickles).

The company changed hands many times, and ended up in 1983 with Dean Foods, which focused the plant on large-quantity production, with up to 500 workers employed at the plant. In 1992, the initial Picklefest was born. Dean Foods closed the plant in 2002, but Picklefest still draws crowds each May.

Home picklers, though, have practiced their craft before and long since. The traditional cucumber-based pickle can find itself in any number of brines - dill, bread and butter, sweet hot and all sorts in-between. In the 21st century, upper-end restaurateurs have rediscovered the pickle, creating overnight pickles to grace burgers, fried okra and chicken.

In Hot Springs, Farnsworth Foods produces Le Pikl, a crunchy sweet pickle with a tiny bit of spicy bite. The company also makes a definitive pickle relish.

Housemade peppery pickles at Smokin' Bull in Emerson.

Caramel apple pie
from Honey Pies
in Little Rock.

PIE

Collectively, the most popular dessert in Arkansas. Forms of pie range from fruit to nut, cream to cream cheese, chocolate, meringue and combimations there-of. Throughout this book, you'll find recipes for Company's Comin' Pie, pecan pie, PCP (pineapple coconut pecan pie) and sweet potato pie. Fried pies are also popular; there's a recipe on the Fried Pie page and another under Old Fashioned Chocolate Fried Pies. For more information on where to find pie, seek out my fourth book, *Another Slice of Arkansas Pie: A Guide to the Best Restaurants, Bakeries, Truck Stops annd Food Trucks for Delectable Bites in The Natural State* (2018).

THE PIG LICKER

Created and shared the first time at the 2008 Arkansas State Fair, this is a strip of bacon dipped in chocolate.

PIGMEAT SANDWICHES

In northeast Arkansas, particularly in Blytheville, barbecue is pork butt, and the sandwiches served at a handful of long-standing barbecue shops, stands and joints in the city are meaty, vinegary and consistent. The oldest purveyor in the city is Dixie Pig, which has been serving pork bar-becue since 1923. Other locations offering this delicacy include Yank's Barbecue, Kream Kas-tle and Benny Bob's.

PIMENTO CHEESE

Arkansas gold is a longtime go-to for home cooks looking for something to fill the lunchbox, but it's gained popularity in recent years as dip and even a condiment for burgers.

Many places have their own pimento cheese recipes, and I've seen all sorts of things in them. This one is my particular version, which my friends (sometime derogatorily) call "Kat food" because of my propensity to bring it along in an old Miracle Whip jar and eat on white bread when working too hard to make dinner on long events.

Kat's Pimento Cheese Spread

8 ounces sharp Cheddar cheese, shredded
2 Tablespoons Miracle Whip salad dressing (NOT mayonnaise)
1-2 ounce jar sliced pimentos in water
½ teaspoon salt

Drain pimentos, reserving pimento "juice." Blend together said "juice," Miracle Whip and salt. Fold in cheese. Immediately place in airtight container and refrigerate. Makes spread for 4-5 sandwiches.

The pimento cheese burger at The Root Café in Little Rock.

Capital Bar and Grill in Little Rock has become famous for many things since its opening in 2007. One of its best known is its pimento cheese and soda crackers. Here's the recipe.

Capital Bar and Grill Pimento Cheese

1 lb. of sharp cheddar
Splash of cider vinegar
¾ cup roasted peppers, pulsed or chopped (drained first)
2 Teaspoon onion powder
2 Teaspoon garlic powder

1 Teaspoon Dijon mustard
¾ cup mayonnaise (Start with ½ cup and add as needed)
Pinch of cayenne
Dash of sriracha

Combine all ingredients in a mixing bowl. Adjust to personal taste. Serve with homemade crackers and peeled celery stalks.

Capital Bar and Grill Soda Crackers

4 cups all-purpose flour
1 Teaspoon baking powder

3 sticks butter
1 1/3 cups milk

Combine the flour and butter in a food processor and pulse until the butter is well cut into the flour. In a mixing bowl, combine the flour mixture with the milk, adding a little flour if it feels too wet to handle. Wrap in plastic and allow to chill for a couple of hours. On a well-floured board, roll thin, "dock" the dough by creating perforations with a dinner fork. Brush the dough with a light egg wash or clarified butter, sprinkle with sea salt and cut to desired size and shape. Bake at 350 F until lightly-browned.

PIZZA

Bruno's Little Italy in Little Rock lays claim to bringing pizza to Arkansas. Every region in Arkansas has pizza of some sort. Some are good, some are great, some are legendary. The pies here mostly come from transplants, in one way or another, including our most established pizza joints.

Tommy's Famous A Pizzeria

Tommy's Famous A Pizzeria in Mountain View has for many decades been considered Arkansas's great hidden pizza. Tommy Miller, a former bodyguard for Elvis Presley, moved to the area after his boss perished. He raised a family in his long, low pizza bungalow on the east side of town, where he brought together Chicago sauce on a Detroit crust for something found nowhere else. Though he has passed on, his family keeps slinging pies.

The Steffey family moved their entire operation from Delmont, Pennsylvania to Lavaca. Glenn and Ruth Steffey started their first Steffey's Pizza in 1963. He was also a trucker, and spent a great deal of time in Arkansas and Oklahoma. A friend convinced him this was a great area in which to live, so in 1980 the Steffeys packed up and moved, opening the second Steffey's in 1971. Read about their signature pizza under Uncle Roman.

Nima's Pizza

The world's second-best pizza, as determined at the International Pizza Challenge, would be Nima's Pizza in Gassville. Jane and Rick Mines have taken second place in the contest four separate times. They serve the classics, but also share many of the great pies that have

ZaZa Fine Salad and Wood Fired Pizza Co.

DeLuca's Pizzeria
Napoletana

won them fame, such as a Reuben-inspired corned beef and sauerkraut pie; an award-winning Spinach pie with roasted garlic white sauce, spinach and cheese; and their most popular, the flowering pepperoni pie with its meatball sauce and cheese-filled pepperoni topping.

There are others, from Little Rock's favorite thin crust at Iriana's to Bentonville's innovative Oven and Tap, biscuit-thick crust at Rod's Pizza Cellar in Hot Springs to the new upstart Sauce(d) in West Little Rock and Fayetteville's own Mo-Jo's Pints and Pies, Arkansas-born franchises like Damgoode Pies, Gusano's and U.S. Pizza Company. And there's Little Rock's own Napoli style high-heat, wood-fired local ingredient packed and beloved ZaZa Fine Salad + Wood Fired Pizza Company.

Then there's this guy who some have called "Mr. Pizza." Anthony Valinoti opened DeLuca's Pizzaria Napoletana in 2013 in Hot Springs and instantly captured the hearts and full attention of pizza lovers in Arkansas. He'll tell you he's not a chef. Valinoti was a muckety-muck on Wall Street, and had spent major time in major cities. After his parents passed, he came up with this idea to start a pizza joint. His sister told him he was crazy. He was planning to start the operation in California, but a friend he caught up with on a trip to Las Vegas directed him to Hot Springs. He booked a flight, got here and declared it home. The Brooklyn native insists on fresh ingredients sourced locally, doesn't have a freezer in the restaurant and greets his clientele in a puff of flour and a soundtrack provided by Bruce Springsteen. Drop in for a high-heat, crusty pie and a whirlwind conversation at his Central Avenue venue.

PIZZA BURGER

A disappearing part of Arkansas's dairy diner menus, the pizza burger was originally created by Paul M. DeAngelis Sr. in 1953 in Muskego, Wisconsin. Unlike "pizza burgers" with dripping marinara sauce and mozzarella sometimes swerved between buns of personal pizzas, these are breaded beef patties with a blend of Italian spices that give the patty the flavor of a pizza. Some come with a bit of marinara between the crust and breading. Older dairy bars still serve this one, including Walker's Dairy Bar in Marked Tree and Shorty's Restaurant in Providence.

PLAY-DE-DO

The official drink of Cajun's Wharf, a Little Rock institution that brings the flavors of Louisiana right to the banks of the Arkansas River. Those who drink from those pink "waters" can take home the jar they came to the table in, a reminder of a pleasant and possibly hazy evening later. I do not purport to know the exact recipe for Cajun's Wharf's Play-De-Do, but I have found a recipe for Play-De-Do, in the book *Prairie Harvest: A Harvest of Recipes* (1981), published by the St. Peter's Episcopal Churchwomen in Tollville, submitted by Martha Bednar of Hazen.

1 part vodka
1 part club soda
½ part light rum
2 parts wild strawberry liqueur
4 parts orange juice
Dash lemon juice
Lemon or orange slices (optional)

Mix all ingredients except slices together and chill. Serve in a tall glass and garnish with lemon or orange slices.

PLUMS

Fleshy, moist and sweet fruit with a pliant skin and a small pit, plums grow well in many parts of Arkansas. It's not uncommon to find Victoria plums that have gone native, growing in woods on what would have been old farmsteads. The pink orbs are ready in June and early July; other, kept cultivars also fruit during the summer months.

POKE SALAT

Indigenous to Arkansas, the large-leaved poke weed is actually considered poisonous, but cooked right (washed, boiled, washed, boiled, etc.) it becomes a beautiful and essential part of the rural experience. Seldom cultivated, poke salat was actually canned by the Allen Canning Company (of first Alma and then Siloam Springs) up until 2000, when it reportedly could not find people interested in picking it wild any longer. It's still found anywhere from the side of the road to forest glens to old homesteads, for those wishing to undertake the making of a mess.

PONE

See Johnnycakes.

Curtis's Botanical Magazine

PORK

Pork chop breakfast at Skyline Café in Mena.

You can't imagine a state that uses the Razorback as its official university mascot without acknowledging pork as a major factor in Arkansas cuisine. It can be found in the barbecue, under a smothering gravy, in its bacon, hams and sausages, chops, chitlins and rinds.

Domestic pork was first introduced to Arkansas by Hernando DeSoto in the 16th century, when he gave European hogs to Native American chiefs as gifts. Some feral hogs known as razorbacks today are believed to be descended from these swine. Arkansas Highway 23 between Huntsville and Ozark became known as "the pig trail" because it was the route farmers used to drive their hogs to market.

While Tyson and Cargill both support feeder pig operations in Arkansas, locally sourced pork can be found at places such as Deep Blue Farms in Hardy and Rabbit Ridge Farms in Bee Branch.

PORK RINDS

Pig skins fried in lard, seasoned, and allowed to air dry. The resultant crisp, curled skin is a popular snack usually purchased like potato chips. Many restaurants have started making them in-house and serving them fresh, such as Delta Q in Forrest City.

POSSUM PIE

If Arkansas had to choose just one particular dessert to represent itself, this would be it. In fact, in both *Arkansas Pie: A Delicious Slice of The Natural State* and in *Arkansas Life* magazine, I put forth the case for possum pie to be named the state dessert of Arkansas. Well, Legislature, what are you waiting on? The dish, by the way, is a pie made with a "sandy" crust (flour, butter and pecans) with a bottom layer of cream cheese filling and a top layer of whipped cream. Chocolate custard, sandwiched between, "plays possum" -- a surprise to the diner who cuts into the pie.

Possum Pie

1 ½ stick butter
2 cups crushed pecans, separated
2 cups flour
1 8-ounce package cream cheese, room temperature

12 ounces Cool Whip, divided
1 cup confectioners sugar
1 box milk chocolate instant pudding
1 box chocolate fudge instant pudding
3 cups milk

Heat oven to 350 degrees. Cut butter into flour to make crumbly pastry dough. Add 1 cup crushed pecans. Press into two eight or nine inch pie pans or one 13" x 9" casserole. Bake 15 minutes or until flour starts to brown. Remove and cool.

Cream together cream cheese and confectioners sugar. Add six ounces of Cool Whip and beat until fluffy. Spread over bottom of both pies.

Blend together both pudding mixes with milk. Pour in on top of the cream cheese mixture and allow to set.

Spread remaining Cool Whip over the top of both pies and sprinkle with pecans. Serves 16, if you're lucky.

Possum pie at The Old South Restaurant in Russellville.

POTLIKKER

The liquid left behind after boiling greens or beans, seasoned with salt and pepper, smoked pork or smoked turkey. Pot liquor, as it's also known, contains essential vitamins and minerals including iron, vitamin C and vitamin K. Often sopped with cornbread, johnny cake or biscuits.

POT-O-BEANS

Barbecue baked beans are a standard side for barbecue all across the state. One Hot Springs classic elevates them to a worthy entrée. At Stubby's Hik'ry Pit BBQ in Hot Springs, navy beans are cooked with ham chunks and sauce in the bottom of the smoker – where they're also subjected to the drippings from smoking hams and briskets above. Each pot is amply doused with more Stubby's sweet, thick sauce before serving.

PRESERVES

As jelly is made from fruit juice, and jam is made from fruit and fruit juice, preserves are fruits combined with sugar and canned (put in jars) to be preserved for future use. In general, preserves are made from whole or sliced fruit and sugar, usually through boiling of said fruit in a simple sugar syrup until it reaches a somewhat candied state. House of Webster makes several varieties of preserves, which are perfect to pair with butter to top biscuits.

ELVIS PRESLEY

It would be odd to create a compendium of Arkansas eats and not mention the state's most famous customer. From the morning he was conscripted into the Army, where he grabbed a cuppa at the Coffee Cup in West Memphis, to his early days touring with The Browns and dining at the family's Trio Club in Pine Bluff, to the many stops he made at Russellville's Old South Restaurant on his way to gigs out west, Elvis left his mark (and his tip) on Arkansas's food scene. Many of our restaurants bear his likeness on their walls; one, in Jonesboro, even shares his last name (though the original Presleys of Presley's Drive-In on Gee Street were actually distant cousins of The King). Because of those stops, some of our restaurants have been added to the National Historic Register.

PRICKLY PEAR

A cactus native to the southern and eastern United States, its paddle-like, spined pads spout flowers in the spring before growing oval, scarlet fruit called tuna. Both the fruit and the pads (nopales) are edible. The soft center of the fruit tastes sort of like watermelon.

Prickly pear makes a great jelly and can be infused into a sugar syrup to add to beverages. Sliced and boiled nopales are called nopalitos; they're marvelous in tacos and scrambled eggs and have a flavor similar to green beans. Take care to remove the long spines and skin before consuming.

Grav Weldon

PULLEYS

Pulleys are the v-shaped chicken part that covers the wishbone. While most restaurants have gone to serving their breasts whole, Neal's Café in Springdale still dismembers its own chickens, and cuts its breasts in three — two sides and the center cut.

Pulleys with red hot apples, apple salad, squash and rolls at Neal's Café in Springdale.

Pulleys with sides at Neal's Café in Springdale.

PUMPKINS

The popular orange or white gourds have been cultivated in Arkansas for more than 4000 years. The flesh within is perfect for baking, and the seeds, when they are roasted, make great snacks.

Several Arkansas farms grow this indigenous orange squash popular with the harvest festival and Halloween crowds, including Motley's in Little Rock and Peebles in Augusta.

PUMPKIN PIE

A popular holiday dessert, usually served with copious amounts of whipped cream or Cool Whip.

1 can (15 ounces) pumpkin
1 can (14 ounces) fat-free
   sweetened condensed milk
2 eggs, slightly beaten
2 teaspoons ground cinnamon
½ teaspoon ground ginger

1 teaspoon ground
   nutmeg
½ teaspoon salt
1 unbaked deep
   dish pie crust

Preheat oven to 425 F. In a large bowl, combine filling ingredients, mixing well. Pour into pie crust. Bake 15 minutes at 425 F. Reduce oven temperature to 350 F and continue baking 35-45 minutes or until knife inserted in center comes out clean. Let cool before cutting. Refrigerate leftovers.

Cravings by Rochelle
in Eureka Springs.

PURPLE COW

Refers to both a collection of classic eateries located in Little Rock, Hot Springs and Conway, and to its eponymous milkshake.

The original Purple Cow location was opened in 1989 by restaurateurs Ed Moore and Chef Paul Bash (*see* Jacques and Suzanne's), who decided to put a high-quality take on the '50s era dairy diner. It proved an instant hit. The interior of each one includes a low bar with stools, milkshakes poured into fluted glasses from metal mixing cups, and lots of nostalgia.

The ice cream for this perineal Arkansas favorite comes from Yarnell's., headquartered in Searcy. This hand-dipped purple permeated vanilla ice cream is a favorite with kids in both milkshakes and ice cream sodas.

See also Ice Cream.

PURPLEHULL PEAS

This variant on the crowder or black-eye pea is originally from Africa, but it's made its permanent home in Lower Arkansas, where it's a very popular summer side dish. PurpleHull peas are similar to black-eye peas but are green with a distinctive spot; the peas grow in a long purple pod, and shelling those peas can strengthen thumbs and turn thumbnails purple.

Celebrate the pea and have a shell of a time at the annual Emerson PurpleHull Pea Festival and World Championship Rotary Tiller Races. This recipe from Christine Snider was the winner for Best PurpleHull Peas at the festival in 2007.

PurpleHull Peas

5-6 cups shelled PurpleHull peas
6 ounces center-cut smoky
   bacon (use a good brand)
Salt to taste

Cut bacon into inch size pieces and lightly brown in a Dutch oven or deep saucepan. Do not drain bacon grease. Add washed peas and enough water to cover plus one inch. Add 2 teaspoons salt. Boil over medium heat until tender (about 45 minutes). Taste and add more salt if needed. Serve with hot buttered cornbread.

Another version comes from Dorothy Dailey of Emerson, who conjured this one in 1990 as a healthier alternative.

Heart Healthy PurpleHull Peas

1 quart PurpleHull peas   1/4 cup cooking oil
1 Tablespoon salt   1/4 cup sugar

Fill a two quart sauce pan half-full of water. Place on high heat. Add salt, cooking oil and sugar. Bring to a rolling boil. Add peas. Bring back to a rolling boil, then turn down heat to a simmer. Cover and cook peas on simmer for 90 minutes.

And this version won Best Salsa at the festival in 2007.

PurpleHull Pea Caviar

1 can PurpleHull peas, drained
1 can black beans, drained
1 can Shoe Peg Corn, drained
1 can water chestnuts, drained and finely chopped
1 can Ro*Tel Tomatoes

1/2 jar pickled jalapeño peppers (12 oz. jar)
2 bunches green onions
3 Roma tomatoes (chopped)
1 bottle (16 oz.) Zesty Italian dressing
Salt and pepper to taste (optional)

Thoroughly mix all ingredients together and toss with Italian dressing. Marinate mixture overnight in refrigerator. Great for football tailgating or snack time served with scoop chips!

Each year, the Emerson PurpleHull Pea Festival and World Championship Rotary Tiller Races bring thousands to the tiny town just a few miles north of the Louisiana border. Over the course of the last weekend in June each year, competitions are held to determine the best pea dish, pea salsa, cornbread and peach cobbler. The area's best shellers vie to see who can shell the most PurpleHull peas in timed trials. There's the Pea Feast of peas, cornbread and peach cobbler; the Million Tiller Parade, and of course the tiller races. Competitors have come from all over the United States and even a few foreign countries to race their tillers along a special dirt track as the community watches. Wipe-outs are common when the tillers get too fast for the runners behind them. The evening wraps up with a street dance.

Fried quail at Murry's Restaurant near Hazen.

QUAIL

A handful of farms in Arkansas's Boston Mountains (the stretch of the Ozarks between Alma and Fayetteville) raise this small fowl for the table. It's served up at several locations around the state, including at Murry's Restaurant near Hazen.

Buttermilk Fried Quail

8 to 16 quail, cut in half
4 cups water
¼ cup kosher salt
2 cups buttermilk
2 Tablespoons Italian seasoning, or
  1/3 cup of chopped fresh herbs
  such as oregano, thyme and parsley

2 teaspoons paprika
1 Tablespoon garlic powder
1 teaspoon cayenne
2 cups flour
1 Tablespoon salt
3 cups vegetable oil

The day before, make a brine with the kosher salt and water. Submerge quail in brine for four hours. Pull out and allow to dry on paper towels.

Mix the buttermilk with all spices except salt. Coat the quail with the mixture and set in a covered container in the refrigerator overnight.

When you are ready to fry, pour the oil into a Dutch oven and heat to 425 degrees. Remove quail from buttermilk and let drain in a colander. Put flour and salt in a ziptop bag and shake.

Drop a few quail into the bag and shake to coat. Remove from bag and place in hot oil. Fry for four to five minutes. Turn over and fry another three to four minutes. Remove from oil and place on a cooling rack over paper towels. Repeat with remaining pieces. Serve hot.

RABBIT

Did you know we have the largest rabbit meat manufacturer in the United States in Rogers? Pel-Freeze began with a rabbit named Betsy Ann, a pet given to Herman Pelfrey's son all the way back in 1911. The pregnant rabbit soon multiplied into an overabundance of rabbits, and the H. F. Pelfrey Company was born. Pel-Freez came to Arkansas in 1947 via Robert Dubbell, who married into the Pelfrey family and moved the operation here. Rabbits have recently become a new culinary focus for many Arkansas chefs.

Rabbit and Dumplings

2 rabbits	Salt, black pepper
1 cup chicken broth	Dumplings (recipe below)
Water	

Place the rabbits in a large pot. Add chicken broth, then add enough water to barely cover the rabbit pieces. Season to taste with salt and pepper. Simmer until the meat is tender and falling from the bones. Transfer to a plate or bowl, allow to cool, and remove the meat from the bones. Discard bones.

Return rabbit meat to the pot, and bring liquid to a simmer. Add previously prepared dumplings. Cover; boil gently for 8-10 minutes or until broth has thickened.

Dumplings:

2 cups all-purpose flour	1 Tablespoon parsley flakes
2 teaspoons baking powder	1/3 cup vegetable shortening
1 teaspoon salt	1/2 cup milk

Combine flour, baking powder, salt and parsley flakes. Cut in shortening. Add enough milk to make a stiff dough. Shape the mixture into a ball, and roll to a thickness of 1/8-inch on a lightly floured surface. Cut into 1-inch strips, and drop into boiling rabbit stock.

Stewed rabbit at South on Main in Little Rock.

RED GRAVY

Sometimes referred to as "Sunday Gravy," this concoction of tomato paste, herbs and broth is the evolutionary point between the traditional bolognase of Italy and the sauce piquant of Cajun country. There's not much difference between this tomato gravy and other tomato sauces. The difference usually comes in the form of a roux on which the gravy is built, or the addition of cream or broth. The Arkansas Delta version of the sauce is a standard over rice, mashed potatoes or biscuits; it's also sometimes used to sauce cabbage rolls. The Faded Rose, a longtime Little Rock mainstay, offers the sauce on mashed potatoes.

Red Gravy From Scratch

1-6 ounce can tomato paste
1-15 ounce can tomato sauce
1-15 ounce can crushed tomatoes
2 cups beef broth
¼ cup red wine (dry)

1 cup finely chopped white onion
1 Tablespoon garlic, minced
Salt and pepper to taste
Olive oil

In a large pot, sauté onion in olive oil until translucent. Add in garlic and let brown. Whisk in tomato paste and beef broth. When heated through, slowly whisk in sauce, crushed tomatoes and red wine. Season to taste. Allow to simmer very low heat to thicken, at least 20 minutes. Serve over biscuits, potatoes or rice.

Quick and Dirty Red Gravy

4 Tablespoons bacon or sausage grease
3 rounded Tablespoons flour
2 cups water

½ small can tomato paste (3 ounce)
Salt and pepper to taste

Stir flour into grease with a whisk over medium-high heat to create a roux. When it has browned to a caramel color, pour water into skillet. Continue to whisk. Add tomato paste and whisk until fully incorporated and gravy has thickened to your liking. Remove from heat. Add salt and pepper to taste.

RED-EYE GRAVY

A roux of ham drippings and black coffee. Some say the thin gruel got its name from the fact that when it sits in a bowl it looks like a big red eye, since the coffee tends to go to the bottom. Others say former President Andrew Jackson requested ham with gravy as red as his cook's eyes. One way or another, this is the only traditional gravy I know that's caffeinated. Chef Matthew McClure at The Hive at 21c Museum Hotel in Bentonville offers this recipe.

Ham Hock Stock

2 medium (1½ pounds) ham hocks
1 yellow onion, roughly chopped
1 carrot, roughly chopped
1 celery stalk, roughly chopped

8 cups chicken stock
1 bay leaf
3 thyme sprigs
1 dried guajillo pepper

In a four quart saucepan, combine all the stock ingredients and bring to a boil. Reduce the heat and simmer, covered, until the hocks are tender, two to 2½ hours. Remove the ham hocks and strain the stock. Return the stock to the pan and reduce to two cups, 25 to 30 minutes. Once cool enough to handle, pick the meat off the hocks and set aside, discarding the skin and bones.

Red-Eye Gravy

2 Tablespoons lard
2 Tablespoons all-purpose flour
2 cups reduced ham hock stock
2 Tablespoons sorghum syrup

2 Tablespoons espresso
Ham hock meat
1 Tablespoon apple cider vinegar
Cayenne pepper, to taste

In a medium saucepan, melt the lard over medium heat. Add the flour and cook, stirring with a wooden spoon, until blond in color, two minutes. Slowly pour in the stock and stir until smooth. Add the sorghum syrup and espresso, and bring to a simmer. Cook, stirring occasionally, until thickened, 20 minutes. Remove from the heat and stir in the reserved ham hock meat and the vinegar. Season with cayenne. Serve over biscuits, topped with fried eggs (optional).

REUBEN SANDWICH

A vast number of Arkansas restaurants carry this popular sandwich, which always includes corned beef and cabbage. Variants around Arkansas sometimes substitute pumpernickel or wheat bread for the customary rye and yellow mustard or 1000 island dressing for the Russian dressing.

Some of the state's best-known restaurants have stellar examples of the sandwich, such as Little Rock's Capital Bar and Grill, Presley's Drive In in Jonesboro, Sparky's Roadhouse in Eureka Springs, the IDK Café in Bentonville, even the cafeteria below the Arkansas State Capitol building. Of course, you can get one at Oaklawn Park, a variation on the facility's famed corned beef sandwich.

This recipe for the Reuben, from *Historic Hot Springs Collections, A Cookbook* (1987) by Judy Giddings and June Simmons, came from the venerated and now lost Mollie's Restaurant.

Mollie's Restaurant Reuben

2 slices rye bread
2 slices Swiss cheese
Sauerkraut, drained

1000 Island dressing
3 ounces corned beef

Spread 1000 Island dressing on each slice of rye bread. Place kraut on each side and cover with Swiss cheese. Add corned beef and close sandwich. Grill with butter on each side.

A Reuben at the IDK Café in Bentonville.

Ribs and fry plate at McClard's Barbecue in Hot Springs.

RIBS

In Arkansas, ribs are primarily pork, and they usually get a dry rub. Razorback Ribs in Yellville and Herman's Ribhouse in Fayetteville are famed purveyors, as are Neumeier's Rib Room in Fort Smith, Brothers BBQ in Heber Springs, Mean Pig BBQ in Cabot, White Pig Inn in North Little Rock, and Rivertowne BBQ in Ozark. Arkansas-based barbecue chain Whole Hog BBQ also claims theirs best.

Our love of ribs is certainly a rubbing off of Memphis and its penchant for ribs, butts and all parts of the hog. My friend Leif Hassell utilizes a similar style, with a combination rub and shake.

Leif's Rib Rub

8 Tablespoons brown sugar, packed
2 Tablespoons kosher salt
1 Tablespoons chili powder
½ teaspoon garlic powder
½ teaspoon rosemary, fresh ground
½ teaspoon cumin, fresh ground

½ teaspoon thyme, rubbed
¼ teaspoon basil, crushed
¼ teaspoon black pepper,
   freshly cracked
¼ teaspoon onion powder
¼ teaspoon cayenne pepper

Combine ingredients thoroughly and seal in airtight container.

Leif's Dry Rib Shake

2 Tablespoons Hungarian paprika
2 teaspoons kosher salt
2 teaspoons black pepper, fresh
   cracked
2 teaspoons garlic powder

2 teaspoons onion powder
1 teaspoon oregano, crushed
1 teaspoon cumin, fresh ground
½ teaspoon chili powder
¼ teaspoon cayenne pepper

Combine ingredients thoroughly and seal in airtight container.

RIB SEASONING

Woody and Cecelia Wood started Woody's BBQ in Waldenburg as a sideline to cropdusting in the mid 1980s. Today, the couple still makes and sells Woody's Dry Rub and Barbecue Sauce, famed for use on ribs, roasts and pork butts from their barbecue trailer at the four-way stop.

RICE

Arkansas produces 51 percent of all the rice grown in the United States. It's exported to lots of other countries, including China. Cultivation of rice here only stretches back about 200 years, but it's caught on and is now a mainstay, especially in the Delta from Crowley's Ridge westward. It's served as a side dish and as part of many other dishes here in Arkansas. For breakfast, sugared rice is an old-fashioned staple. Rice with brown gravy is common, as is rice pudding.

Riceland Foods is the world's largest miller and marketer of rice. Based in Stuttgart, it produces large number of rice products, from mixes to a fine rice bran oil which does marvelously as fish fry oil.

Another Stuttgart facility, Producer's Rice Mill, puts out Par Excellence rice and blends, including the marvelous Garden Harvest, which includes not only rice but dehydrated vegetables and herbs.

Ralston Family Farms offers sustainable, artisanal rice grown in the Arkansas River Valley milled fresh, with varieties from golden to white to jasmine brown.

Stuttgart is considered the Duck and Rice Capital of the World, and for good reason. Its place at the heart of the Grand Prairie isn't just perfect for growing rice; those ducks love the swamps, fields and water available in this area.

Stuttgart was founded by a German immigrant, George Adam Buerkle, a Lutheran minister who arrived in Ohio in 1852. In 1878 he purchased seven thousand acres on the vast expanse in the heart of the Arkansas Delta and recruited a colony of 48 men, women and children to the site. The next year he brought in the second colony – which included his family – and sold what he didn't keep himself to the new residents at the same price he'd paid – just $3 an acre. He named the new community after his hometown, thus Stuttgart was born.

The town didn't really take off until the late 1880s, when the railroad was first pushed up from Gillett to the south. Stuttgart was incorporated in 1889, and its first mayor was Colonel Robert Crockett – who happened to be the grandson of the famed frontiersman Davy Crockett. The area's industry focused on furniture making, wagons, blacksmithing, woodworking and farm implements, and several dairies and even a soft drink plant were established there.

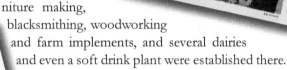

But the town's destiny blossomed in 1902, when Bill Hope planted the first plot of rice as an experiment. Even though folks kept "sampling" the plot for souvenir rice plants, it produced wildly – with 139 bushels per acre. Rice took off in the area, and the Stuttgart Rice Mill Company was incorporated in 1907. In 1921 a band of farmers formed a cooperative and created what is now Riceland Foods, the world's largest miller and marketer of rice. A second company, Producers Rice Mill, was established in 1943 and continues to produce impressively.

The city quickly expanded during the second World War with the U.S. Government's purchase of a large number of rice fields north of town and the establishment of an airbase. In addition to using Stuttgart-area rice to feed troops, the airbase was utilized to house German prisoners of war during the conflict.

Today, the town still boasts a population of nearly 10,000 – a number that increases two- to five-fold each November as duck season opens. In 1936, the Wings Over The Prairie Festival was created to celebrate ducks and duck hunting, and today it's host to the annual World Championship Duck Calling Competition, which draws in competitors from all over the world. Private duck lodges bustle throughout the fall and winter months, while farming is the focus of spring and summer.

ROLLS

A popular option for bread to accompany dinner, the yeast risen starch comes in many varieties. White versions include Brown `N Serve rolls, trefoil and even clover leaf rolls. Other versions, such as brown wheat, rye, and Hawaiian sweet rolls are sometimes offered. Not to be confused with biscuits.

This recipe for clover leaf rolls comes from the AQ Chicken House in Springdale, originally published in *Where To Eat In The Ozarks* by Ruth M. Malone (1961). AQ, of course, stands for Arkansas Quality.

Clover Leaf Rolls

Bring to boil one cup milk, cool to lukewarm with one cup water, then add 1/2 cup melted Crisco. Dissolve two cakes compressed yeast in 1/4 cup warm water, then combine with 1/2 cup sugar and an egg in mixer. Add milk and water and about eight cups flour and 1 1/2 teaspoon salt. Mix for eight minutes. Let dough rise. Then divide dough into small balls. Place three in each greased muffin cup and let rise again. Bake 20 minutes at 350 degrees. Makes two dozen rolls.

RO*TEL

The 1943 invention of Carl Roettele, who was afraid folks wouldn't be able to pronounce his name on a product. Roettele opened his Ro*Tel plant in Elsa, Texas in 1943, canning more than 25,0000 cases of vegetables a year. His blend of tomatoes and chili peppers would reach Arkansas in 1956, which would in turn give Arkansas home cooks the ability to create a version of cheese dip by pairing the product with Velveeta quickly and easily (recipe under Cheese Dip). Ro*Tel appears here because in 2010, the year of the inaugural World Cheese Dip Championship, Ro*Tel representatives let slip that more folks bought original Ro*Tel inside Arkansas, than outside Arkansas.

SALSA

A sauce of chopped, uncooked vegetables or fruit used as a condiment? Arkansas has more than its share of salsas. While most focus on the traditional trio of tomatoes, onions and peppers, some restaurants offer more innovative versions. For instance, Local Lime (with locations in both Little Rock and Rogers) offers six versions - house tomato, a Caribbean mango, a warm Tres Chiles with Arbol and Pasilla peppers, Verde Tomatillo, a chipotle version with sultana raisins and pineapple, and a smooth zucchini with pumpkin seeds.

Versions of salsa have been on menus in Arkansas since the first Ark-Mex restaurants opened; we've come a long way from the thin, pureed versions that resembled little more than tomato juice. Chunkier, spicier, thicker and more complex versions are the norm these days.

Central Arkansas folks know they can get a really good mild or spicy version from Robbi's Salsa. Very close in flavor to the old JR's Restaurant variety from the 1980s, Robbi's is rich and thick. Northwest Arkansas has spurred the creation of My Brother's Salsa, which covers a spectrum of flavor with Black Bean and Corn, Cranberry Orange, Tomatillo and Fire Roasted options.

SAUSAGE

A link or patty of ground and spiced meat, usually pork but sometimes buffalo, beef or turkey, served with breakfast. Sausage is often utilized in the making of gravy, and biscuits with sausage gravy are considered a hearty breakfast in and of themselves. Sausage is a common breakfast side. For those wishing to make their own, Townsend Spice and Supply in Melbourne covers everything from cures to casings.

SAUSAGES

Meat ground, spiced and forced into casings, then smoked or cured. Usually served sliced, though small sausages can simply be enjoyed as they are. The act of preserving sausages has been maintained over the ages as an Ozark custom. Versions can be found hanging, ready for purchase at Coursey's Smoked Meats in St. Joe. Petit Jean Meats in Morrilton offers several varieties in grocery stores and via online ordering, including one that's a combination of venison and pork.

SASSAFRAS

When I was a young girl, I recall my paternal grandmother treating stomach ailments with sassafrass tea. I learned how to spot the leaves in the woods, and I remember watching her digging roots of a small tree at the back of her huge garden. I also remember trips into the Ozarks, where sassafras candy would be procured and carefully rationed over coming months. I loved that flavor.

Sassafras tea is a beverage once drank in the spring to thin the blood. In the spring, the roots are still full of sap, which makes a better tea. In *High on the Hog, Lickin' Good Eatin' Hillbilly Recipes*, Ella Mae Tucker shares how to find and prepare the roots.

"Dig the roots of the sassafras tree. Young tender roots or the bark from the old roots are washed clean and cut into lengths which will fit into a pan. Cover well with water and bring to a boil. The amount of the water can be a lot or a little, depending upon how many you plan to serve, how fresh the roots are, or whether you plan to hold a strong brew in the refrigerator, and weaken it with water later, as desired...serve hot or cold, with or without sugar."

SETTLERS' BEANS

Also referred to as Calico Beans, this is a combination of beef and bacon, tangy sauce and beans. This is my mom's recipe.

1 pound ground beef
1 large onion, chopped
1 pound bacon
¼ cup brown sugar
½ cup sugar
½ cup barbecue sauce

½ cup ketchup
4 Tablespoons sorghum molasses
2 (16 ounce) cans navy beans
2 (16 ounce) cans pork and beans
2 (16 ounce) cans chili beans

In a skillet, brown ground beef and onion. In another skillet, fry bacon. Drain both. In a five quart pot, stir together brown sugar, sugar, barbecue sauce, ketchup and molasses. Add in beef, bacon, onion and beans and simmer on low heat for one hour.

SMOKED CHICKEN

Behind pork ribs and butt and beef brisket, a popular choice for barbecue in Arkansas. Birds are usually smoked half or whole and served with traditional barbecue sides - coleslaw, potato salad, fried okra, mashed potatoes or macaroni and cheese. Found all over the state.

SMOKED HAM

See Ham.

Half chicken at Old Post Bar-B-Q in Russellville.

SMOKED TURKEY

Alden Burge achieved some small-town fame by smoking chickens and turkeys in his backyard for football Friday nights in Lewisville after relocating there from Shreveport back in 1953. His smoked birds became so popular, he bought the local dairy bar in 1962 and turned it into his family's smoked turkey headquarters to meet demand. A second location was opened on R Street in Little Rock's Heights neighborhood in 1979. In 2010, Jack Burge sold the store to Jeff Voyles, who still runs the restaurants and the company today.

Burge's sells thousands of turkeys, mostly in November and December, both online and at the store. The richly brined and smoked birds are so popular, it is not uncommon to see a line out the door for people picking up orders the week before Thanksgiving.

See also Turkey Salad.

Grav Weldon

SMOKED SIRLOIN

Fred and Lou Gaye retired to Bella Vista in 1969. Fred had been a petroleum engineer, and the couple had moved about quite a bit – spending time in 13 different countries. When it came time to settle, the couple decided to chase a lifelong dream. They purchased a couple of acres along Walton Boulevard in Bentonville called the Wildwood Camp. Though the camp was in disrepair, Lou saw value in it, and renovation began. In 1970, Fred's Hickory Inn was opened. Fred smoked the meats and Lou created the side dishes. The restaurant became a favorite of Walmart founder Sam Walton. He threw his wife a surprise 60th birthday party there, and his brother Bud is believed to have agreed to donate the money for the University of Arkansas's arena during a dinner at the restaurant. President Bill Clinton, before he made his announcement in 1991 on his intention to seek the presidency, shared his plans during a retirement party on the premises. Images of the dozens of celebrities who have passed through the doors - including Jonathan Winters, Garth Brooks, Paula Abdul and Denver Pyle - are posted on the walls in the foyer.

The restaurant has changed hands a few times over its nearly 50 year history, but it still offers a hickory smoked sirloin - tender, flavorful, served with a marvelous jus. Its dry-rubbed edges provide texture and even more flavor to savor.

SMOTHERED CHICKEN

Similar to rice with brown gravy, this is a concoction of long-stewed chicken in its own gravy, served over rice. Alternately, a boneless fried chicken section covered in chicken gravy. Here's a recipe.

1 pound chicken thighs	1 teaspoon smoked paprika
1 1/2 cups all purpose flour	1/4 cup vegetable oil
1 teaspoon salt	2 cups chicken broth
1 teaspoon ground black pepper	1 cup whole milk
1 teaspoon celery seed	2 teaspoons minced garlic
1 Tablespoon onion powder	1 medium sized onion, chopped
1 Tablespoon garlic powder	

Pour 1 1/2 cup flour into a large bowl, and add in all dry seasonings. Mix well. Coat chicken with this seasoned flour, and make sure you coat all surfaces. Reserve seasoned flour.

Pour oil into a large skillet, then place over medium heat. Add in chicken when oil is hot. Remove when crust is golden brown.

Add onions to remaning oil in skillet. Sautee for two minutes, then add minced garlic and cook a minute more. Remove. Add three tablespoons of the reserved seasoned flour and stir in to make a roux. Once incorporated, whisk in first the broth, then the milk. Let it cook together about three minutes.

Remove bones from chicken thighs. Add chicken to skillet with onions and garlic. Make certain chicken is completely covered in the gravy. Cover and allow to cook for 30-35 minutes, turning occasionally. Serve over rice.

SNOW ICE CREAM

Arkansas is a four season state, with a judiciously long summer and long "shoulder seasons" in fall and spring. Winter can be bitterly cold, but snowfalls of more than an inch are an event that close schools and roads. Ample snowfalls of four or more inches rarely happen more than three or four times a winter.

Because of this, we celebrate our snow. Every first snow of the season, I receive requests for this recipe. My friend Polly Murphy once pointed out to me that snow ice cream wasn't a thing elsewhere, and I think she's right.

Snow Ice Cream

2 gallons clean fresh snow
1 (14 ounce) can sweetened
  condensed milk

1 cup milk
1 cup white sugar
1 teaspoon vanilla extract

Pour snow into a large bowl. Stir condensed milk, milk, sugar, and vanilla extract together in a bowl until smooth. Pour milk mixture into snow, stirring until completely combined. Freeze for at least an hour.

SOAKED SALAD

See Italian Soaked Salad.

SOFT SERVE ICE CREAM

Arkansas is dotted with dairy diners, many of which have been in service more than half a century. From the Dairy Dip in Mulberry to the Dairy Freeze in Fort Smith, Big John's Shake Shack in Marion to the Daisy Queen in Marshall, soft serve ice cream is the perfect summer accompaniment, whether in a cone or cup or on pie.

SOP

The act of soaking up a substance such as gravy or juice with an absorbent matter like bread or cornbread. Alternately, the substance being sopped by said absorbent matter. *See* Gravy *and* Potlikker.

SOPAIPILLAS

A very popular Mexican dessert in the mid 20th century, these puffs of dough have become much rarer to find. The delicate flour pillows were on the menu at Mexico Chiquito, Casa Bonita and several other Ark-Mex restaurants of the time. Savvy diners knew to best savor them, you tore a corner off a sopaipilla and drizzled honey directly into the cavity within. A sticky yet satisfying mess.

Casa Bonita Sopaipillas

2 cups flour
1/2 cup cold water
2 Tablespoons Crisco shortening
2 teaspoons baking powder
1 teaspoon salt

4 cups vegetable oil
Confectioners sugar (optional)
Honey (optional, but you will want it
  anyway)

Sift together flour, baking powder and salt. Cut in shortening until the mixture resembles crumbs. Add water and wait two minutes. Kneed water into crumbs. If after two more minutes the mixture is dry, add water one tablespoon at a time until it forms into a rollable dough. Roll into a ball, cover with a towel and let rest 30 minutes.

Roll dough flat. Cut into square or rectangular surface. At this point, you can either fry them or freeze them (freezing instructions below).

In a deep skillet, heat oil to 400 degrees. One by one, slip dough squares into hot oil with a wooden spatula. Dough will puff immediately. Once the dough is golden on one side, turn it to cook on the other side. Each one will take about 30 seconds. Lift by edge with tongs and place on paper towels to drain. DO NOT EAT IMMEDIATELY. The puffed dough will be full of hot steam. Let rest five minutes. Dust with powdered sugar if you chose. Serve with honey.

To freeze for later: after cutting dough, set squares on a cookie sheet lined with wax paper. Put in the freezer for two hours. Remove dough from wax paper and store squares in freezer bags. To prepare for frying, lay dough squares out in a single layer for at least 30 minutes or until no longer frozen. Proceed with directions as suggested.

Sorghum molasses being procured and processed at Parker Pioneer Homestead near Harrisburg.

SORGHUM MOLASSES

Sorghum molasses on biscuits is a rite of passage for young Arkansawyers. Long a sweetener for dishes, many of our city-raised kids never have the experience of their first bite of sorghum molasses on a biscuit.

Sorghum molasses, or sweet sorghum molasses, is made from sorghum cane, which is pressed for its juice. That juice is then boiled down and filtered and reduced to a thick syrup consistency, when it then canned for preservation. It was a popular sweetener up until just after World War II. Making sorghum molasses is very labor-intensive, and when farm labor decreased after the war, sorghum operations ceased producing the syrup. Sorghum has continued to be planted as a cover crop and food for animals; a new effort to utilize milo (grain sorghum) as a gluten-free grain alternative is gaining traction in Arkansas.

See also Milo.

Not to be confused with molasses, a viscous by-product of refining sugarcane or sugar beets into sugar.

SOYBEANS

More soybeans are grown in the United States than anywhere else in the world. Arkansas ranks 10th in the nation in soybean production. Most soybeans grown here go to animal feed, but local chefs are using the bean in some food applications. Arkansas version tends to be a bit sweeter than that grown in Asia, thanks to a difference in soil components.

See also Edamame.

Catfish with Soybeans, Corn Mash, Crispy Potato and Hollandaise at the Arkansas Soy Supper at South on Main in Little Rock.

SPAGHETTI

Long a tradition of Italian families throughout the state, the long thin noodles have for years been seen drying for months ahead of the Tontitown Grape Festival, on the racks at Regina's in Lake Village and elsewhere.

This recipe was published years ago and passed around, and has been credited to Mama Z's in Tontitown. The name tied to it is that of one Mrs. Arch Featherston.

Mama Z's Spaghetti Sauce

1 large onion, chopped
1 cup chopped celery
1 pound ground beef
1 15 ounce can tomato sauce
1 6 ounce can tomato paste

1/2 teaspoon salt
1 teaspoon oregano
garlic to taste
1 4 ounce can mushrooms
1/4 pound Parmesan cheese, grated

In heavy pan, brown onion, celery, and meat. Drain. Add tomato sauce and tomato paste, salt, oregano and garlic. Cover and simmer over low heat several hours, stirring frequently. Add cheese and cook until cheese is melted. Serve over cooked spaghetti.

Spaghetti with meatballs at Angel's Italian Restaurant in Hot Springs.

If you're going to have traditional spaghetti, you might also want meatballs. This recipe comes from Edna Zulpo and was originally printed in *Restaurant Recipes of the Ozarks* (JE Cornwell, Judie Cornwell, Tom Dease, 2006)

Mama Z's Italian Meatballs

2 lbs. lean ground beef
1 teaspoon salt
1/2 teaspoon black pepper
4 cloves garlic or 1 Tablespoon
   minced garlic

1/4 cup dried breadcrumbs or oats
2 eggs, beaten
4 Tablespoons finely chopped onion
2 Tablespoons finely chopped celery
2 Tablespoons dry Italian seasoning

Mix all ingredients except ground beef. Add ground beef to mixture and mix. Do not overmix as it will make your meatballs tough. Roll 1/4 cup of meat mixture into a ball. Makes about 16 meatballs.

Place meatballs in a baking dish and bake 35-45 minutes on 350 degrees. Add meatballs to spaghetti sauce in saucepan and simmer on low heat for approximately 30 minutes before serving.

Mama's Special Italian Plate at Mama Z's in Tontitown.

CAPITAL HOTEL'S SPICED PECANS

Considered the "front porch of the South," Little Rock's famed Capital Hotel has hosted dignitaries and boasts two of the best recognized restaurants in the city, One Eleven at the Capital and the Capital Bar and Grill. The hotel, which has served the River City since 1870, boasts an impressive foyer with its original tile, an elevator that's big enough for horses, and a reputation for extraordinary lodging experiences. The spiced pecans, often gifted to guests and available at the Capital Bar and Grill, have become a beloved flavor of the city.

3 1/4 cups water
3 cups granulated sugar
1 pound pecan halves
2 teaspoons finely ground kosher salt

1/4 teaspoon cayenne pepper
Oil for frying

In a medium saucepan, simmer sugar in water until completely dissolved. Add pecans. Increase heat gently to boiling. Allow to boil 10 minutes. Remove from heat. Remove pecans and allow them to dry on paper towels.

Heat oil in a deep fryer until the temperature reaches 375 degrees. Toss salt and pepper together in a separate bowl and set aside.

Place pecans in fry basket. Fry in oil 30-40 seconds. Remove from oil, quickly drain and then toss them in bowl with salt and pepper. Spread on cookie sheet and allow to cool completely. Store in jars in a cool place.

SPINACH

The Allen Canning Company in Alma once produced 65 percent of the world's canned spinach and claimed a place as Spinach Capital of the World, complete with park and statue of cartoon character Popeye the Sailor Man. Dozens of Arkansas farms still raise spinach, though Allen Canning Company has relocated to Springdale. Alma still celebrates its spinach connection with the annual Alma Spinach Festival each April.

SPIRO'S GREEK DRESSING

Spiro's was a mainstay in Texarkana for generations, known for baklava, an excellent dish of trout, and this dressing, which some would put on crackers.

1 large jar of mayonnaise
  (NOT Miracle Whip)
1 medium sized white onion

4 cloves of garlic
4 boiled eggs
1 Tablespoon paprika

Place all ingredients in a blender and puree to desired consistency.

SPOON BREAD

A soft, moist dish of cornmeal, eggs and milk that can be served as a savory side dish or a dessert component, similar to cornbread but with a much wetter consistency. It gets its name from being so soft, you should eat it with a spoon.

This is Ruth Powell's recipe from *Recipes From Arkansas: Compiled by Members of the Arkansas School Food Service Association* (1977).

Heat to boiling point two cups milk. Add corn kernels shaved thin from six ears of corn. Stir in 2/3 cup cornmeal and one teaspoon salt. Continue to stir constantly and cook mixture five minutes. Remove from fire. Beat in 1/4 pound (1/2 cup) butter and one tablespoon sugar. Beat together three egg yolks and two cups milk, then add to mixture. Beat until stiff and dry three egg whites. Fold into mixture. Fill buttered baking dish. Bake 60 minutes in moderate oven (350 degrees F). Serve immediately. This spoon bread is delicious when served with fried chicken and cream gravy.

SPUDNUTS

The original Spudnuts were the creation of Al and Bob Pelton, two Salt Lake City boys who first encountered potato-flour doughnuts in Germany. They came back to the States in the late 30s and attempted to recreate the addictive rounds themselves – and succeeded with a recipe they started utilizing in 1940 – which became the heart of their Spudnut Shop franchise. Six years later they had 200 stores that utilized their dry spudnut flour in the making of golden rounds. Twenty years after that they were stretched coast to coast with more than 600 outlets.

However, the Peltons sold their company in 1968 to National Oven Products, owned by Pace Industries. Pace turned around a few years later and sold off National Oven Products to Dakota Bake-N-Serv… which itself closed down shortly thereafter. The corporation, its company and Spudnuts the franchise all evaporated with a conviction of fraud and conspiracy in 1979. Franchisees were left holding the bag and most disappeared within 10 years.

But two of the franchises are still in operation here in Arkansas – one in Magnolia, opened in 1959 – and the other in El Dorado, opened in 1948. The two stores have differently styled buildings and different vibes… but they both still sell the golden rings six mornings a week.

SQUASH

An easy to grow gourd fruit related to cucumbers, pumpkins and melons. Several varieties of the plant grow easily in Arkansas. Many varieties are indigenous to Arkansas, and have been elemental in agricultural comunities for centuries. Cultivation dates back more than 9000 years. Varieties include pattypans, yellow crooknecks, cushaws, and zucchini. Squash blossoms as well as the fruit are edible; the fruit itself is fibrous and filling, while the blossoms are a flavorful addition to soups and stews and are themselves stuffable. This recipe by Sue Henderson comes from *Recipes to Remember*, published by the First Assembly of God of DeWitt.(2002).

Squash Casserole

3 medium yellow squash
1 onion, chopped
1/2 cup fine bread or cracker crumbs
1/3 cup shredded Cheddar cheese

1 egg, beaten
1/2 teaspoon salt
1/4 teaspoon pepper
4 Tablespoons margarine, divided

Cook squash and onion in small amount of salted water until tender; drain. Add bread crumbs (reserving one tablespoon for top). Add cheese, egg, salt, pepper, and two tablespoons margarine. Spoon into greased casserole. Top with remaining crumbs and dot with two tablespoons margarine. Bake at 375 degrees for 10 minutes or until brown. Makes four servings.

Fried Squash Blossoms

15 large squash blossoms, rinsed
   and dried
1 large egg
1/2 cup sparkling water

1 1/2 cups all-purpose flour
1/2 teaspoon salt
Pinch of fresh ground nutmeg
3 cups oil for frying

Remove the stem, pistils or stamen inside of each flower Separate the eggs. Set the whites aside. In a large mixing bowl, lightly beat the yolks. Stir in the sparkling water, then slowly whisk in the flour, salt, and nutmeg. Beat the whites with an electric hand mixer until they form soft peaks, then fold into the mixture.

Heat oil in a deep skillet. When hot, dip each flower in batter mixture, letting any excess batter drip off, then fry, turning until light golden brown. Be careful not to crowd the pan. Drain briefly on paper towels, sprinkle with salt and serve.

SQUIRREL

Arkansas is known for many fine delicacies… but one of its strangest consumables has to be, without a doubt, squirrel. This wild game that was once a last desperate choice for poor hunters to bring to the table has been elevated to the star attraction at one of our odder food events – the World Championship Squirrel Cookoff. The brainchild of Joe Wilson, a construction project manager in the area, started off in 2012 as a way for the town of Bentonville to remember its rural roots. Native squirrels have a great habitat in the Arkansas Ozarks, and to these aficionados, they go by many names, such as "tree bacon" and "limb chicken." Promoters for the event site the animal as all-organic. The annual celebration allows competitors to show off how they can best prepare and share this alternative to "the other white meat." Each entrant sets up his booth, decorated with their best squirrel-hunting gear or themed items. The squirrel is cooked, brought to judges, and a winner is determined. Each cook can make anything they want from their squirrel, as long as the meat within the dish is 80 percent squirrel. The event has drawn attention from outside the state, including a 2013 visit from Andrew Zimmern of Travel Channel's "Bizarre Foods America."

STEAK

The 33 ounce Porterhouse for Two at Taylor's Steakhouse near Dumas.

Arkansas celebrates steak each year with the World Championsip Steak Cook-Off in Magnolia. Several restaurants have become defined for their remarkable beef steaks, particularly in the Arkansas Delta. Here are five steaks you should encounter when you're in the eastern third of the state..

Originally opened by Charles and Dorothy Taylor in a shotgun-style house west of Dumas in 1954, over four moves and 58 years, Taylor's went from country grocery to lunch counter and liquor store, before son Chuck and his wife Pam turned the whole operation around in 2012. Today, enjoy Chuck's remarkable 28 day dry aged Kansas City bone-in ribeyes, filets, and gigantic Porterhouse steaks.

Pine Bluff's venerable Colonial Steak House opened in 1973 on the bottom floor of a 1912 schoolhouse. Currently owned by Dana and Wayne Gately, the eatery's Roast Prime Rib of Beef is a gorgeous chunk of beef meant for a couple.

At The Tamale Factory, a restaurant in a horse barn near Gregory, T-bone and Porterhouse steaks start at two pounds and get larger from there. George Eldridge's establishment is named for the tamales made in-house for the eatery and his other operation, Doe's Eat Place in Little Rock - also kown for great steaks..

In West Memphis, the prime rib at Bourbon Street Steakhouse within Southland Gaming and Racing is incredible. And savvy upper Delta diners know to get over to Jerry's Steakhouse in Trumann for the Sweetheart Special, where couples receive both a large and a small ribeye dinner for one price.

See also Beef.

Roast Prime Rib
of Beef at
Colonial Steakhouse
in Pine Bluff.

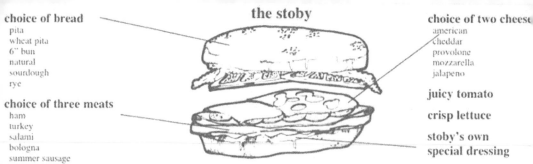

the stoby

choice of bread
pita
wheat pita
6" bun
natural
sourdough
rye

choice of three meats
ham
turkey
salami
bologna
summer sausage

choice of two cheese
american
cheddar
provolone
mozzarella
jalapeno

juicy tomato

crisp lettuce

stoby's own
special dressing

The STOBY

A sandwich featuring your choice of bread, three meats and two cheeses with special sauce, popularized at Stoby's in Conway and Russellville. The meats include ham, smoked turkey, Petit Jean summer sausage, Petit Jean salami or Petit Jean bologna; cheeses to select from are American, Swiss, Cheddar, Mozzarella, Provolone or Pepper Jack; and you can have the combination on a pita, a wheat pita, a bun, whole wheat bread, sourdough or marble rye. The Stoby is really anything you make it.

STRAWBERRIES

From late April through mid-June, the food focus is on the sweet-tart ripe red berry. Restaurants such as Brave New Restaurant in Little Rock and the Bulldog Drive-In in Bald Knob create strawberry shortcakes; the Rock Café in Waldron serves up strawberry cobbler; and thousands of young folks will have fingers turned red after picking their own, or picking up a quart or two at places like Holland Bottoms Farm in Cabot.

Freezer-Preserving Strawberries

As a child, two memories have stayed with me regarding strawberries. One involved picking berries from the strawberry plants my maternal grandmother put out and getting into a world of trouble. Those berries were bitingly tart, but still juicy enough to leave that red tell-tale stain on my lips. Any jury would have convicted me.

The other memory comes from how those strawberries were preserved. Once I was older and more trustworthy, I could assist in the picking of strawberries. Each berry was washed, capped and sliced and packed into a Cool Whip tub. Each tub in turn would be topped off with a cup of sugar or more, and the lid secured. Those that went to the refrigerator came back out within hours or days, and they'd magically created a syrup coveted atop butter cake (*see* Butter Cake) or shortcakes. Those that went to the freezer showed up throughout the year for incorporation in congealed salads, cake fillings and topping for ice cream.

Sugar isn't necessary for preserving strawberries, I would come to later learn. To properly freeze them, one needs freezer space, cookie sheets and patience as each berry is washed, dried, set separately on the sheet, frozen and then shaken into gallon-sized freezer bags for preparation throughout the year.

STRAWBERRY COBBLER

A delicious dessert that's been on the menu at the Rock Cafe, which has served Waldron since 1936. The crust and fruit combination has for the last several years spread through the western part of the state. Seasonal to late spring and early summer.

STRAWBERRY SHORTCAKE

Ripe strawberries sliced and served in their own juice on a shortbread with whipped cream and sometimes other embellishment. The shortbread can be substituted with sponge cake or pound cake, but it's essential the juice that gathers with the strawberries after they've been sprinkled with confectioners sugar be included in the serving.

No place better utilizes the fruit than the Bulldog Restaurant, a dairy diner which serves the plump, syrupy berries over a cookie-like shortbread with whipped cream (and ice cream on request) only during months when the berries are fresh from local fields. Food lovers schedule special trips to Bald Knob for the succulent experience, sometimes hailed as the opening salvo of spring's first harvests.

STUFFED BAKED POTATOES

A rather popular way of consuming shredded barbecue in Arkansas, this method requires baking a potato, splitting it open and piling the insides with barbecue and sauce, along with additional optional embellishments such as baked beans, coleslaw, cheese, or sour cream.

Several varieties exist around Arkansas, from the choose-your-own-topping versions at Ralph's Pink Flamingo BBQ in Fort Smith to the encased-in-sauce option at Stubby's Hik'ry Pit BBQ in Hot Springs.

Stuffed baked potato at Ralph's Pink Flamingo BBQ in Fort Smith.

Stuffed baked potato at Stubby's Hik'ry Pit BBQ in Hot Springs.

STUFFING

Shame on you. Go see Dressing.

SUMMER PLATE

Almost every person I know my age or older who spent any time in rural Arkansas, craves the apex of heat in our mid-year, not for that heat but for the lunchtime meal we would savor and share together: the summer plate.

As a child, it was the essence of humility, simply leftover cornbread and peas and whatever my maternal grandmother had picked that morning: fresh corn cut off the cob, sliced juicy tomatoes, sliced cantaloupe, chunks of white onion. If one of us had gone out that morning and caught a mess of bream or perch, and if it wasn't too hot yet, Grandma Bear might take the cleaned fish and fry it on one burner. Otherwise, the oven stayed off.

It was humble, but it was also wondrous. There'd be margarine or butter that had been left to soften on the counter to spread on chunks of cold cornbread. Chow chow, green tomato relish, maybe even some pepper jelly would be on the table, alongside salt and pepper. She'd set everything out before we got in from whatever we were doing - adults from the yard, kids from picking berries or yanking weeds or having adventures in the veritable forest that was her circular wildflower garden amidst sunflowers and African violets. I didn't know we were poor... how could we be, with feasts such as these?

Other lunches in the summer were different. In the city, it was conveniences like sliced bread, luncheon meat and New York Sharp Cheddar cheese. On a fishing trip, it was potted meat, saltine crackers and Miracle Whip. At childcare it was three things-from-a-can, apple juice and disappointment. But I was a city girl, and by the time I was a teenager summer lunch was drive-thru fare, TV dinners and whatever I came up with from the pantry. By adulthood, summer plate was gone.

Over the course of researching Arkansas food, my mind has been drawn back to those ideals again and again. In 2018, the desire to return to this tradition seems to have come to a head with several of us in the food community. I sat down with

Scott McGehee, he of such restaurants as Local Lime and Heights Taco and Tamale in Little Rock, to discuss the idea. He too has fond memories of the summer plate, experienced at the table of his grandmother, Ruby Thomas of the Red Apple Inn around Heber Springs.

There were many similarities in our experiences. Both our families celebrated the bounty of the garden with fresh fruits and vegetables harvested before the heat of the day drove everyone inside. There was often fried fish, and cornpone. What separated our families in our dining situation, appeared to be economics. Ruby Thomas' summer plate included items that had been cooked in an oven, or on the stovetop, without the concern of heating the house. Her table might have fried okra or beans from a hot pot.

A summer plate created and photographed by Scott McGehee.

Fellow Arkansas food writer Rex Nelson once shared his perfect meal of the summer - one where, as a boy, he would catch fish with his grandfather, and no matter how small they were, they were good enough to eat. His grandfather would clean the fish, his grandmother would fry it, and with it they would dine on fresh tomatoes and vegetables from the garden, fried potatoes, cornbread and peas. His rural roots in Arkadelphia were not far from my weekends outside of Gurdon, a short distance away, and our tables were similarly set.

McGehee, Nelson and myself have been known to bemoan the fact that outsiders look in on us for our outrageous dishes - cheese dip, fried pickles, and chocolate gravy - skimming on the sensational rather that looking for what we really eat. As time passes and generations pass, I fear the summer plate could fade. It is, in the end, the one dish that appears all over Arkansas, a single uniting idea that brings us to savor our bounty at the height of its glory, which truly deserves notice.

SUNFLOWERS

A popular garden addition, that produces sunflower seeds which, in turn, are the source of sunflower oil. The Wayne Plantation, founded in 1889 in Scott, is in its fourth generation. The family grows NuSun Mid Oleic Sunflowers, which produce an all-natural, non-GMO cold pressed extra virgin oil full of Vitamin E. In recent years, the oil has become extremely popular.

SWEET CORN

See Corn.

SUGARED RICE

A popular breakfast option for past generations of Arkansawyers, this is simply rice with sugar and butter. In 2007, Chef Lee Richardson brought the idea back to the table with housemade rice grits at Ashley's at the Capital (now superseded by One Eleven at the Capital). Rice grits have appeared on menus in many upscale restaurants; at least one Arkansas company is working to create a product for home use.

SWEET POTATOES

Indigenous to the Americas, these tubers are mild to deep orange in color and are used in casseroles, pies and as a side dish, often glazed with brown sugar. Plant sweet potatoes in May, and your first harvest will come about 100 days later. They must be pulled before the first killing frost; once they're out of the ground, they can last for up to six months in dry storage. This is my mom's recipe.

Sweet Potato Casserole

2 eggs
1 cup sugar
3/4 cups margarine or butter
1/2 cup milk
1 teaspoon vanilla

3 cups sweet potatoes,
   cooked and mashed
1 cup brown sugar
1 Tablespoon margarine or butter
1/3 cup flour
1 cup pecans, chopped

Blend eggs, sugar, first margarine or butter, and vanilla. Add to sweet potatoes and place in a 12" x 7" baking dish. Mix brown sugar, second butter or margarine, and flour, making fine crumbs. Place on top of sweet potatoes, then cover with nuts. Bake at 350 degrees for one hour.

Pies on display at the Say It Aint't Say's Sweet
Potato Pie competition at the annual Mosaic
Templars Cultural Center Open House in Little Rock.

SWEET POTATO PIE

Little Rock's Sweet Potato Pie King, Robert "Say" MacIntosh, popularized the longstanding dessert for decades through his own efforts and through restaurants he ran. Today, his pies are celebrated with the annual "Say It Ain't Say's" sweet potato pie contest each December at the Mosaic Templars Cultural Center in Little Rock.

I cannot even pretend to make a sweet potato quite like Say's, but I do have this recipe, and it's not bad.

Sweet Potato Pie

1/3 cup butter, softened
1/2 cup sugar
2 eggs, lightly beaten
3/4 cup evaporated milk
2 cups baked sweet potatoes,
   peeled and mashed

1 teaspoon vanilla extract
1/2 teaspoon ground cinnamon
1/2 teaspoon ground nutmeg
1/4 teaspoon salt
1 pie crust, blind baked

Cream butter and sugar. Add eggs and mix well. Add milk, sweet potatoes, vanilla, cinnamon, nutmeg and salt and keep stirring until incorporated. Pour into pie crust. Bake at 425° for 15 minutes. Reduce heat to 350°; bake 35-40 minutes longer or until a knife inserted near the center comes out clean. Refrigerate until ready to serve.

TAMALES

Brought to Arkansas from Mexico, reinterpreted by a Sicilian merchant living in eastern Arkansas, augmented in a soul food café and ingrained in the soul of the Arkansas Delta -- the tamales on this side of the Mississippi River tends to be made with beef (and sometimes chicken) rather than the pork version served on the other side. The delicacy's roots in Arkansas hearken back to the 19th century, in particular Peter St. Columbia, a Sicilian who came to America and eventually settled in Helena, learning tamale-making from Mexican immigrants who worked the fields. His son would share the recipe with the family who ran a soul food restaurant in one of his buildings during the Great Depression. His grandson, Joe St. Columbia, still sells tamales based on the recipe tweaked through the decades, as Pasquale's Tamales from a trailer alongside US Highway 49 in West Helena.

At Rhoda's Famous Hot Tamales and Pies in Lake Village, these soft masa cylinders are filled with chicken fat, beef and spices. Rhoda Adams and her family still pack them two dozen to a coffee can for those who want to take them home for freezing. Chicken is the filling of choice for Lackey's Tamales, the Cajun-seasoned wonders from Clint Lackey's original recipe, still sold at Smokehouse BBQ in Newport. And George Eldridge of Doe's Eat Place has the famed tamales sold at that place made in a barn on his property in Gregory, which he opens each Friday and Saturday night as The Tamale Factory.

Arkansas Delta-Style Tamales

1 (6-ounce) package dried corn husks   1 teaspoon chili powder
cornmeal dough (see next page)   1 teaspoon ground cumin
chicken filling (see next page)   2 1/2 quarts water
1 (15-ounce) can tomato sauce

Soak corn husks in hot water to cover one hour or until softened. Drain husks, and pat dry. Spread two tablespoons cornmeal dough into a three by five inch rectangle on one side of one husk, leaving a two-inch border at bottom narrow edge and a 1/2-inch border at one long side.

Spoon two heaping tablespoons chicken filling down center of cornmeal dough rectangle, creating a one-inch-wide strip. Roll husk up, starting at the long side with 1/2-inch border, enclosing meat filling with the first turn. Fold bottom end with two-inch border over, and secure with kitchen string or strip of softened corn husk. Repeat procedure using remaining cornmeal dough and chicken filling.

Bundle together six filled corn husks, seam sides inward and open ends facing same direction, and secure with kitchen string. Repeat procedure with remaining filled corn husks, making two more bundles of six filled corn husks each.

Stand all three corn husk bundles, open ends up, in a large 12-quart stockpot. (If the bundles won't stand upright in the stockpot, place a two-cup glass measuring cup upside down in the stockpot for the corn husk bundles to rest upon.)

Stir together tomato sauce, chili powder, and cumin. Pour tomato sauce mixture and 2 1/2 quarts water around corn husk bundles in stockpot. (Do not pour directly over corn husks.) Cover and bring to a boil over medium-high heat. Reduce heat to low, and simmer, covered, three hours. Remove tamales, discarding tomato sauce mixture.

Cornmeal Dough

2/3 cup vegetable shortening
1 1/2 cups yellow cornmeal
1 cup warm chicken broth

2 teaspoons salt
1 teaspoon paprika

Beat shortening at medium speed with an electric mixer five minutes or until light and fluffy. Stir together cornmeal and warm chicken broth in a medium bowl until well blended. Gradually add cornmeal mixture to shortening, beating at medium speed just until blended after each addition. Add salt and paprika, beating just until blended. Cover dough with plastic wrap, and set aside until ready to use.

Chicken Tamale Filling

3 cups finely chopped cooked chicken
1 (4.5-ounce) can chopped green chiles
2 teaspoons garlic powder
2 teaspoons onion powder

1 teaspoon chili powder
1 teaspoon salt
1/2 teaspoon ground red pepper

Stir together all ingredients.

TEA

Arkansas food without a glass of iced tea is almost inconceivable (save, of course, dairy bar food, which goes well with Grapette). We brew thousands of gallons every year, to chill and to serve over ice. While sweet tea has become predominant across the state in recent decades, brewing tea and adding sugar to the entire batch is a relatively recent concept begun commercially in the 1980s. Before that, tea was served unsweetened, and if you wanted it sweet, you were directed to the sugar bowl.

TOFFEE

David Smith started out making pecan toffee for holidays for friends and family. When he started managing the Red Apple Inn, owner Patti Upton asked him to start making it to sell at Aromatique's shop. He and his wife Nancy went from there to candy shows in Dallas and Atlanta and in 2002 started selling his product as Red Apple Inn Southern Pecan Toffee. The company grew so fast that David and his wife Nancy founded Lambrecht Gourmet Toffee five years later. Their award-winning artisan chocolate covered toffees are mouth-watering and addictive and come in oh so many flavors.

Then there's Debbie's Gourmet English Toffee, made with pure cane sugar. The milk chocolate enrobed toffee is available by the pound out of Fayetteville.

TOMOLIVES

While working on pickled products for the Atkins Pickle Plant in the early 1950s, Robert Switzer came on a new idea - pickling tiny green baby tomatoes. The resulting Tomolives became a popular addition for mixed drinks. The little globes taste a lot like pickles, but with more salty punch.

TOMATOES

The Bradley County pink tomato is Arkansas's state fruit and vegetable, but many other varieties are found each year in gardens all over the state. Tomatoes have been in Arkansas since at least the early portion of the 19th century, and grace everything from sauces to salsa, but are, in my honest opinion, best eaten whole and raw in-season.

See also Bradley County Pink Tomatoes.

TRACE CREEK POTATOES

A potato dish created at and offered by Brown's Country Store and Restaurant in Benton. The dish, which bears some similarity to potatoes au gratin, combines a cheesy sauce with potato slices and a cornflake crust.

TORTILLAS

Round corn and flour tortillas have long been available in Arkansas. In Dardanelle, Tortilleria Morelos has been operating for decades to provide fresh tortillas to restaurants and customers in the area.

In Bentonville, Mamma Z's Tortilla Factory opened in January 2018 by Rosalba and Luis Zepeda. It provides tortillas for many area restaurants, including Modern Biscuit, Yeyo, the Purple Banana food truck, and Local Lime. Unlike other operations in the state, the Zepedas use only whole organic corn in red, blue, white and yellow, which they process with hydrogen peroxide utilizing nixtamalization, a culinary technique that utilizes an alkaline substrate in order to process and cook corn. The resulting product is preservative and gluten-free and non-GMO to boot, and takes about 21 hours from kernel to tortilla. At Mamma Z's, colors in tortillas and chips come only from plant matter - peppers for red, kale for green, and beets for purple.

TROUT

Introduced to Arkansas and popular in its rivers, especially the White River and Red River in northern and eastern Arkansas. Several species of trout populate the cold waters below the Greers Ferry Dam, Bull Shoals Dam and other areas in Arkansas, including brown trout, rainbow trout and cutthroat trout.

To fish for trout in Arkansas, one not only needs a fishing license, but either a resident or non-resident trout permit. Both are available online through the Arkansas Game and Fish Commission (AFGC). They can also be purchased at bait shops and Walmart stores. This recipe comes from AGFC.

Baked Trout with Bay Leaves

1 clove garlic, crushed
1 1/2 teaspoons minced fresh thyme
Black pepper
4 12-inch trout, pan-dressed
4 bay leaves
3 Tablespoons butter, melted
Juice from 1 lemon
3 Tablespoons fresh parsley, minced

Preheat oven to 400 degrees. Combine garlic, thyme and black pepper to taste in a bowl. Place a bay leaf and an equal portion of the seasonings inside each fish. Arrange fish in a single layer on an oiled baking dish.

Pour melted butter over the fish and bake five minutes. Baste with the butter in the dish and bake an additional five to seven minutes. Sprinkle with lemon juice and parsley. Remove bay leaves and serve.

Broiled Trout Italiano at DeVito's Italian Restaurant in Bear Creek Springs.

The DeVito family began operating a trout farm in the Bear Creek Spring community in 1970. It was a gift from Albert Raney, who ran the trout farm at Dogpatch USA, to his daughter Mary Alice and her husband, Jim DeVito, after DeVito retired with 29 years in the service. In 1986, they and their four sons opened DeVito's Restaurant, serving Italian classics and trout dishes made with the fish visitors would catch from the creek. A fire destroyed the original location in 2000. The family rebuilt and continues to serve the Harrison area.

The oldest brother, James, left the family operation to open the equally venerable DeVito's of Eureka Springs in 1988.

TROUT PÂTÉ

A specialty of DeVito's Restaurant at Bear Creek Springs, this is a spread made from smoked trout served on club crackers.

TURKEY

Bred and raised domestically all over Arkansas; also a popular wild fowl hunted each fall and spring. Wild turkey can be taken during a two week period each year in April.

See also Smoked Turkey.

TURKEY FRIES

A dish of dubious contents, purportedly the male parts of a turkey, served alongside calf fries (beef testicles) and dragonfries (stuffed jalapeños) at Cattleman's Steak House in Texarkana.

Smoked turkey from Cross Eyed Pig BBQ in Little Rock,

TURKEY SALAD

Alden Burge became famous for his turkey-smoking skills in the 1950s in the tiny southwest Arkansas town of Lewisville – where he'd prepare the birds before football games. The dairy diner his family purchased there (along with a second restaurant in Little Rock's well known Heights neighborhood) still offers smoked turkey every day in sandwiches, as whole birds and smoked breasts for the holidays, and in this unduplicatable secret-recipe turkey salad, affectionately known as "turkey crack" by regulars. The paste-like smoke-heavy concoction made fresh each day has earned a significant following.

TURNIP GREENS

An incredibly popular rural side item or winter's meal all over Arkansas. Turnips come up twice a year with a late spring crop and a fall crop. The roots are great starchy additions to the diet, while the greens are often boiled down and served up as a side dish.

TURNIPS

A root vegetable beloved not only for its starchy root but for its leafy, delectable greens. Turnips can be planted both in early spring for summer harvest, and in August and September to be harvested as needed throughout the winter months. The latter harvest also means turnip greens are available year-round to enjoy.

The UNCLE ROMAN

A specialty double-crust pizza offered at Steffey's Pizza in Lavaca. Back in the 1950s, Glen Steffey was stationed at Fort Chaffee, where he was a baker. Between Fort Smith and Delmont, PA he developed his very own crust and sauce recipes. He opened the first Steffey's with his wife Ruth there in 1963. In 1980, Glen went to Stiegler, OK to work. He went to visit his friend Don Ray in Lavaca one day, and decided it was where he wanted to set roots. The entire family moved down, and in 1981, Steffey's Pizza opened in the western Arkansas town. Today, Glen's daughter LeAnn operates the place with her husband Shayne and daughter Briar.

The Uncle Roman started off as an early-week buffet item. It didn't take long for it to catch on. Even though it takes 15 minutes longer to cook than the average pizza, it's become popular. It's cooked in a cast iron skillet between two parmesan-dusted crusts. Sauce and cheese glue the whole thing together.

The Uncle Roman

18 ounces pizza dough, divided 10/8	Your favorite pizza toppings
6 ounces pizza sauce	Garlic butter to brush on
12 ounces provolone cheese	Parmesan cheese

Preheat oven to 400 degrees. Grease bottom & sides of a 10" cast iron skillet. Roll out a 10 ounce dough ball and place in bottom of skillet. Press dough all the way up the sides of the skillet. Spread four ounces of pizza sauce on the bottom, then layer six ounces of smoked provolone cheese on that. Add toppings generously, then top with another six ounces of provolone and two more ounces of pizza sauce. Roll out an eight ounce dough ball and place on top of skillet. Pinch dough edges together like with a deep dish pie and brush with garlic butter. Sprinkle Parmesan cheese over the top. Cut vent holes. Bake at 400 degrees for 30 minutes until golden brown.

Venison profiteroles by Chef William Ginocchio
at UAPTC-CAHMI in Little Rock.

VENISON

Indigenous to Arkansas, white-tailed deer are hunted all over Arkansas in the fall months. The meat from this animal is used extensively by the rural population, and it's seen a recent resurgence on the menus at fine restaurants here. This is my mom's recipe, originally published in *Cornerstone Cookery*, edited by Kitty Waldon and put out by the St. Vincent's Infirmary Employee Council in 1984. Everyone has one cookbook they keep going back to. This one is mine.

Venison Chili

1 pound ground beef, browned
   and drained
3 pounds ground venison, browned
   and drained
2 large onions, diced
2 teaspoons paprika
1/8 teaspoon oregano

1 bay leaf
1 clove garlic, minced
1 Tablespoon black pepper
1 Tablespoon chili powder
1 green bell pepper, seeded and diced
1 32 ounce can tomato juice
2 six ounce cans tomato paste

Combine all ingredients in Dutch oven and simmer over low heat for three hours.

WAFFLES

De Wafelbakkers has origins in Holland, and the company's waffles have long been imported to the United States. In 1986, two custom built ovens were installed in the Meyer's Bakery located in Hope to produce the original Holland waffles here. They were so popular, a permanent facility was built in North Little Rock in 1994. Today, De Wafelbakkers manufactures frozen pancakes and waffles, as well as shelf-stable waffles, distributed throughout the United States, Canada and Mexico.

WATERMELON PICKLES

A refreshing condiment that bears sweet and sour flavor notes similar to the medieval Iranian beverage sekanjabin, watermelon pickles have long been a bright, biting Southern condiment of note. It's a chutney-like side item that goes well with grilled meats and in salads. This recipe (in memory of Louise Hall) was published in the *Family Recipe Collection of All Souls Church Aid* in the Scott community in 1981.

Watermelon Rind Pickles

8 lbs. prepared rind
10 lbs. sugar
4 cups vinegar
2 oranges, sliced (rind and all)
2 lemons, sliced (rind and all)
2-3 ginger sticks or powdered
ginger in bags
2-3 cinnamon sticks
2 teaspoons whole cloves
2 gallons water and 1 heaping cup hydrated
lime (more if needed to cover)

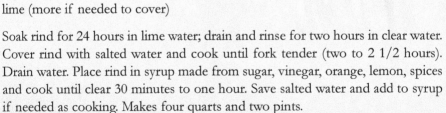

Soak rind for 24 hours in lime water; drain and rinse for two hours in clear water. Cover rind with salted water and cook until fork tender (two to 2 1/2 hours). Drain water. Place rind in syrup made from sugar, vinegar, orange, lemon, spices and cook until clear 30 minutes to one hour. Save salted water and add to syrup if needed as cooking. Makes four quarts and two pints.

WATERMELONS

Sure, other states have watermelon, but Arkansas is home to the sweetest watermelons in the world. A unique layer of limestone running under a layer of sandy topsoil in and around the town of Cave City, added to long hot summers, is believed to produce watermelons with a higher sugar content than those found elsewhere. And the largest watermelons in the world, according to the Guinness Book of World Records, are grown in Hope.

At the Cave City Watermelon Festival each year, area growers donate some of their crop for a community feast, and serve them by slicing up the melons and passing them out. Everyone has as much as they want, and it's all free.

WEINERS

The town of Weiner is situated in the Upper Delta, along US Highway 49 just north of Waldenburg. However, if you're talking about weiners in Arkansas, you're probably talking about the singularly brightest red weiners in the state, produced by Petit Jean Meats. The weiners, which have a non-toxic dye added to their casing, are highly requested. A few years back, Petit Jean Meats attempted to discontinue the product, but consumers begged for their return. In addition to the famed red hot dogs, Petit Jean Meats also makes a plump normal version as well as an all-beef selection.

WHISKEY

Rock Town Distillery is Arkansas's first legal distillery opened since Prohibition. Founded in 2010 by Phil Brandon, the artisan craft distillery uses grains from Arkansas to distill award winning spirits, a true grain-to-glass distillery, with spirits distilled from corn, wheat and rye grown within a 125 miles of its Little Rock distillery. Selections available include vodka, gin, rum, bourbon, whiskey and a popular product called Arkansas Lightning, a type of moonshine. Rock Town Distillery has won numerous international awards for its spirits and can be found in numerous states, the United Kingdom and Canada.

WILD GAME

Arkansas is a hunting and fishing state. It's in our genes; our native inhabitants subsisted on game and items gathered. The explorers who came learned of the customs. The first settlers lived off turkey, elk, bison, deer and the other animals who populated our woods. Elk and bison were hunted to extinction (though elk was reintroduced to Arkansas in 1981), but other game continues to be part of our diet. For hunters in Lower Arkansas and most of the rest of the state, deer hunting is an essential part of rural life; venison is harvested, processed and put up to bring to table throughout the winter months.

Grav Weldon

In the Arkansas Delta, the game of choice is duck, and thousands of hunters will don waders and head out into the Grand Prairie, the Big Woods region and bayous to blinds on early autumn mornings. Other game birds include white fronted and Canada geese, coot, crow, teal, snipe and woodcock.

Hunters may take deer, elk (on a very limited license), alligator, bear, turkey, rabbit, squirrel, and quail with a license and subject to limits. Feral hogs, a nuisance animal not indigenous to Arkansas, have no limit on private lands.

Venison Stew at the Berry Pre-Coon Supper in Gillett.

Some church and community groups cook up wild game dinners as fundraisers. The preparation and sale of wild game at Arkansas restaurants is not permitted.

WICKED MIX

Salty, spicy, sometimes even chocolate-y, this Little Rock-produced snack mix is an easy win to stuff anyone's stocking. Try it in spicy, hot and chocolate-laced varieties, or enjoy new Wicked Minis, seasoned oyster crackers for easy snacking.

WINE

Arkansas's wine country, centered near Altus, is the oldest and largest viticultural area in the South. It first found cultivation for fruit of the vine with rail workers, German and German-speaking Swiss immigrants who labored for the Little Rock and Fort Smith Railroad from 1875 to 1879 in exchange for land grants along the railpath. Two immigrants who toiled on those rails would start wineries in 1880 that still operate today.

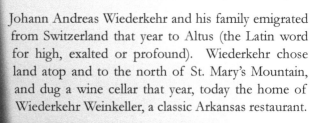

Johann Andreas Wiederkehr and his family emigrated from Switzerland that year to Altus (the Latin word for high, exalted or profound). Wiederkehr chose land atop and to the north of St. Mary's Mountain, and dug a wine cellar that year, today the home of Wiederkehr Weinkeller, a classic Arkansas restaurant.

Jacob and Anna Post also came to Altus in the 1880s, and settled on the farm of Joseph Bachman, a Swiss grape grower. The Posts made wine from both wild grapes and the new varieties. During Prohibition, their daughter-in-law Katherine was sent to jail for making wine. After the ban was lifted, the Posts joined a co-operative, which Jacob purchased in 1951 and renamed Post Winery. Today, it's run by fourth and fifth generation Posts.

The Altus region is also home to Mount Bethel and Châteaux Aux Arc wineries, and Cowie Winery has operated across the river in Paris since 1967. The 21st century has seen a boom in winemaking, with operations popping up all over.

XANTHAN GUM

It's a stretch, but there is a foodstuff that starts with X being used in Arkansas cuisine. Xanthan gum is a common food additive found in everything from sauces and dressings to ice cream and yogurt. It's become a frequent additive of gluten-free baked goods. Xanthan gum is produced through the fermentation of sucrose, lactose and glucose. After fermentation, the resulting moist residue is dried, then ground into a fine powder. When mixed with liquid, the powder becomes viscous and almost gel-like. In gluten-free cooking, it acts as a binder for flour and dough.

It's often used in preparations at Little Rock's gluten-free bakery, Dempsey Bakery. The operation is a labor of love for Paula Dempsey, who decided with her family in 2008 to shut down the longstanding Dempsey Film Company and open a place where those with gluten allergies could dine without worry. The move came after the first member of the family was diagnosed with health issues requiring a gluten-free diet. As more members of the family were found to have the genetic condition that prevented gluten consumption, Paula created something special for those who needed another option. Today the restaurant serves not only cakes and pies but bread, sandwiches, soups and lunches, and boasts an expertly stocked take and make case.

YELLOWBELLY MELONS

These are simply watermelons that have yellow meat inside. Many claim Arkansas watermelons with yellow flesh are sweeter than their pink or red hearted counterparts. They ripen and are usually available in late July and August.

A slice of yellow watermelon at the Cave City Watermelon Festival.

YELLOW SQUASH

Indigenous to Arkansas, grown in Arkansas gardens, this summertime squash varietal was originally cultivated by Native Americans. Yellow squash is the go-to for squash in supermarkets around these parts, It's often served baked, sautéed or fried. This recipe is from *Secrets of the South Volume II, A Collection of Southern Recipes* by Alice May Johnson of Gillett, published in 1995 by Harding Press.

Yellow Squash Bake

1 10 ounce package chopped yellow squash or fresh squash, cooked
1 10 ounce can cream of chicken soup
1 8 ounce container sour cream
1 chopped onion
1/2 cup milk
1/2 cup cracker crumbs
3 cups cooked rice
1 can water chestnuts, drained and sliced
1 cup grated Cheddar cheese (optional)

Cook squash according to package directions, drain and mash. Combine with remaining ingredients except cheese. Spoon into a 2 quart casserole dish and bake at 350 degrees for 30 minutes. Remove from oven, top with cheese. Return to oven until cheese is melted. Serves 6.

Fried Yellow Squash

2 yellow squash
1 cup flour
1 cup oil (for frying)
1 teaspoon salt
1 teaspoon pepper
1/4 cup milk
1 egg

Slice squash into 1/4 inch rounds. Heat oil in skillet over medium heat. Sift together flour, salt and pepper. Beat egg together with milk. Dip all rounds into flour mixture, then dip in egg mixture and dip back into flour. Fry in single layer in skillet until brown on both sides. Dry on paper towels. Serve hot.

YOGURT

Frank Hickingbotham started This Can't Be Yogurt back in 1981 in the Market Street Shopping Center on Rodney Parham - a clean white counter and some soft-serve machines that doled out soft frozen yogurt. At that point in time, there were no frozen yogurt chains. Hickingbotham's creation grew to seven locations in 1982, then 400 in 1986, and over 800 in 1987. A tiff with a similarly-named restaurant in Texas forced a name change to TCBY. After reaching 3000 locations, the chain cut back, and was eventually purchased by Mrs. Field's. Today, there aroue around 475 locations nationwide, including several in Arkansas.

14

ZUCCHINI

The most popular "we have too much of this" vegetable from Arkansas gardens, zucchini is one form of Arkansas squash. It came prominent in American gardens in the 1950s after being reintroduced from Italy.

Italians acquired the zucchini over 300 years ago and formed a liking for it. The name is a derivation of an Italian word meaning "sweetest." Dark green and firmer than its yellow cousin, it grows quite well here, and it's great stewed, baked and even on the grill.

ZUCCHINI BREAD

A popular use for the masses of zucchini that emerge from gardens all over the state. You can't grow just a couple of zucchini - there's probably some sort of regulation against that. The plants are fruitful here, and the fruit in turn is abundant.

Here's a recipe from *Arkansas Heritage: Recipes Past and Present* by the American Cancer Society, Arkansas Division (1992).

Zucchini Bread

3 cups flour
1/4 teaspoon baking powder
1 teaspoon baking soda
1 teaspoon salt
3 eggs
1 cup oil
2 1/2 cups sugar
1 teaspoon vanilla extract
1 teaspoon cinnamon
2 cups grated zucchini
1 cup chopped pecans

Heat oven to 350 degrees.

Sift flour, baking powder, baking soda and salt together. Combine eggs, oil, sugar, vanilla, and cinnamon in mixer bowl; mix well. Add dry ingredients; mix well. Stir in zucchini and pecans.

Spoon into two greased loaf pans. Bake at 350 degrees for one hour. Remove to wire rack to cool.

Yield: 24 servings.

One more crazy recipe...

This dish by Margret Bounds appears in *Red Hot Cooking!* by the Almyra Fire Department Auxillary (1977).

Smothered Fried Beaver

Back legs and tender loin of young beaver
Flour
salt and pepper to taste
oil
onion, thinly sliced
garlic powder

Slice beaver thinly and roll in seasoned flour with salt, pepper and garlic powder. Brown in oil and place in heavy pan alternatinv with onion. Pour enough water to come only to the top layer of meat and cover tightly. Bake in a 350 degree oven for one hour. Tastes like deer steak!

INDEX

Recipes marked in blue

Magnolia Bake Shop is the oldest bakery in Arkansas. Since 1928, it's been owned by the same family. Doughnuts and pies are popular here - but if you go, do yourself a favor and get an Italian cream cake.

Magnolia Bake Shop

If your sweet tooth is acting up, Steve Stroope and all your taste, from gingerbread men to birthday cakes, the fine folks at Magnolia Bake Shop have a mouth- their specialty. Opened in 1928, the family-owned bak-watering array of bakery goods guaranteed to suit, ery is one of Magnolia's oldest businesses.

Every other place in the state, this is called cheese dip. But at Taco Mama's in Hot Springs, it is queso. Diana Bratton hails from Texas, and offers this made from scratch queso. If you ask for it in a molcajete, it'll stay hot your entire visit.

Cherokee Village has a population of over 4600 and just two restaurants in the city limits. Chow on the Square offers gourmet sandwiches, salads and take-home items. Carol's Lakeview Restaurant serves breakfast, lunch and dinner seven days a week at extremely reasonable prices (no standard menu item over $9.99), including single platter-sized pancakes big enough for any appetite.

In comparison, Eureka Springs has around 100 restaurants and bars with a population of 2000. The eateries serve not only locals but the town's hefty tourist base. Some restaurants close in January and February during the slow season - but even then, there are excellent dining options for any price range. Of these, Local Flavor Café is known as the place locals eat, for good reason: the adaptive menu and friendly staff are both admirable.

The oldest restaurant building still in existence in Arkansas is the Hinderliter 2. Grog Shop. The building was built in 1826 in Little Rock by Jessee Hinderliter. He ran it as a tavern - but it earnedits its claim to fame as the last meeting place of the territorial legislature in 1835. It would at one point in time also house a barbecue joint before volunteers began restoring it to its original state, first in the 1930s and then in the 1960s. Today, the structure is part of the complex at the Historic Arkansas Museum in downtown Little Rock.

Skyline Café in Mena has been open since 1922. It was struck by a tornado in 2009, and the contents of the interior were scattered through town. Residents returned almost everything that was lost, and the restaurant reopened six months later. The restaurant still serves some of the best corned beef hash in the state.

Truck stops can often be a good place to find vittles. The Hillbilly Hideout inside the I-40 Travel Center in Ozark has incredible breakfasts, lots of pies and a dish called the Heavenly Hog - an Arkansas version of the Monte Cristo with ham, turkey, American and Swiss cheeses melted between three slices of bread, battered and deep fried, then dusted with powdered sugar and served with strawberry jam.

The largest fried pies in the state can be found at another truck stop, the Bald Knob Phillips 66 Travel Center. There are sometimes as many as a dozen flavors available, including pecan cream cheese, caramel apple, turtle, strawberry cheesecake and even Oreo cheeecake. The stop also offers buffets for breakfast, lunch and dinner and a 24 hour hot fried food counter.

A set-up is when you go to a fish place and get just the fixings - usually hush puppies, green tomato relish, beans, onions, coleslaw and such, instead of a traditional meal. A set-up can be really filling, too. The Fish Net in Arkadelphia and Catfish Hole in Alma both offer the option.

The walls inside Molly's Diner in Warren are covered with witty plaques, bumper stickers and memorabilia. You can spend hours just reading while enjoying your meal.

In Bentonville, you can dine inside a reutilized 1904 church at The Preacher's Son. Chef Matthew Cooper utilizes local produce, meats and grains to create an ever-changing menu of South meets Pacific Northwest delights, many of which are gluten-free.

This roadside stop along Arkansas Highway 74 east of its junction with Arkansas Highway 23 is a delightful spot for a summertime picnic. A small parking area, a few picnic tables and access to a spring from the rock face, plus the shade from that edifice from the south, allows for cool breezes and a comfortable respite from the drive.

Bill Clinton weighs a chicken at an Arkansas Poultry Federation event.
Courtesy Shiloh Museum of Ozark History/Arkansas Poultry Federation Collection

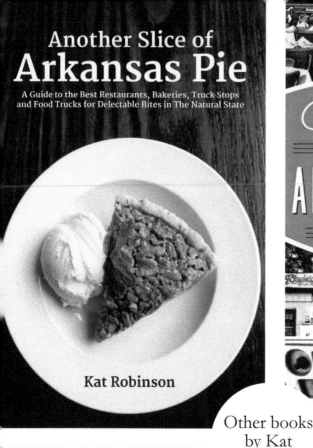

Another Slice of
Arkansas Pie

A Guide to the Best Restaurants, Bakeries, Truck Stops
and Food Trucks for Delectable Bites in The Natural State

Kat Robinson

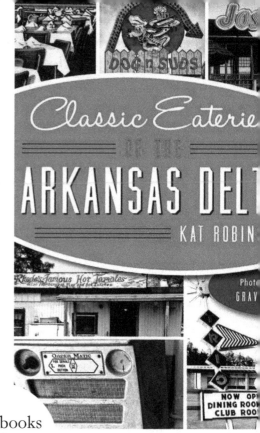

Classic Eateries
OF THE
ARKANSAS DELTA

KAT ROBINSON

Rhodes' Famous Hot Tamales

Photo
GRAV

NOW OP
DINING ROO
CLUB ROO

Other books
by Kat
Robinson

OARK
CAFE

Classic Eateries
of the OZARKS and
ARKANSAS RIVER VALLEY

KAT ROBINSON

Majestic

PAUL'S
Bakery

KAT ROBINSON
photography by
Kat Robinson & GRAV WELDON

Arkansas
Pie

A
DELICIOU
slice of
NATURAL
STATE

ACKNOWLEDGMENTS

This book encompasses eleven years of research and a lifetime of being surrounded by Arkansas cuisine. It would not exist without the assistance and encouragement of others.

To Kerry Kraus, Jack Heinritz and Leif Hassell, my proofreaders and fact checkers. Thank you for making sure what is presented here is factual, grammatically correct and makes sense.

To Thomas, Ruth and Grace Pepler of Dogwood Hill Guest Farm, much appreciation for providing me with many of the foods photographed in this book, for the feeding of this author and for the encouragement along the way.

To Scott McGehee for the conversations. Your insight has been extraordinarily valuable, especially with providing a contrasting view on Arkansas food.

To Patti Stobaugh and Sharon Woodson. You kept me going when I was frustrated, and insisted that yes, this book needed to be written.

To Sara Willis, Mona Dixon and the folks at the Arkansas Educational Television Network. I am gratified by your encouragement.

To Max Brantley, who ten years ago offered me the chance to explore Arkansas's foodways and cuisine under the Eat Arkansas banner at the *Arkansas Times*.

To Vicki Vowell, Heather Baker, Caleb Talley and the rest of the gang at *AY Magazine*, thanks for sharing my voice as Arkansas's food expert.

To Beverly Sanders, who helped me dig into the culinary roots on the paternal side of my family and reclaim some of the flavors of my youth.

To my mom, Kitty Waldon, who compiled and published my favorite cookbook, *Cornerstone Cookery*, when I was my daughter's age. I never knew how much your experience would settle with me, and I understand more of what you went through to create that book, which contains so many of the recipes that are part of my own culinary lexicon.

And to Grav Weldon, who throughout the writing, shooting and layout of this book made sure I was fed, had everything I needed to be comfortable, and provided me with feedback and the reassurance I wasn't crazy for attempting such an immense project.

Kat Robinson is Arkansas's food historian and most enthusiastic road warrior. The Little Rock-based travel writer is the host of AETN's *Make Room For Pie; A Delicious Slice of The Natural State* and a committee member for the Arkansas Food Hall of Fame. The author of *Arkansas Food: The A to Z of Eating in The Natural State*, Kat has also compiled the comprehensive travel guide for pie lovers, *Another Slice of Arkansas Pie: A Guide to the Best Restaurants, Bakeries, Truck Stops and Food Trucks for Delectable Bites in The Natural State*. Her other books are *Arkansas Pie: A Delicious Slice of the Natural State*, *Classic Eateries of the Ozarks and Arkansas River Valley*, and *Classic Eateries of the Arkansas Delta*. She is the Arkansas fellow to the Southern Food and Beverage Museum, and the 2011 Arkansas Department of Parks and Tourism Henry Award winner for Media Support.

Her work appears in regional and national publications including *Food Network, Forbes Travel Guide, Serious Eats, AAA Magazines* and *AY Magazine*, among others. While she writes on food and travel subjects throughout the United States, she is best known for her ever-expanding knowledge of Arkansas food history and restaurant culture, all of which she explores on her 1200+ article website, *TieDyeTravels.com*.

Before jumping into the world of food and travel writing, Kat was a television producer at Little Rock CBS affiliate THV and Jonesboro ABC affiliate KAIT, as well as a radio producer and personality for KARN Newsradio.

Kat lives with daughter Hunter and partner Grav Weldon in Little Rock.

For questions about Arkansas food, travel, or how to book a talk with Kat, email her at *kat@tiedyetravels.com*.

CPSIA information can be obtained
at www.ICGtesting.com
Printed in the USA
BVHW022148250219
541168BV00008B/31/P

9 780999 873434